ROBERT BURNS

After the painting by Alexander Nasmyth

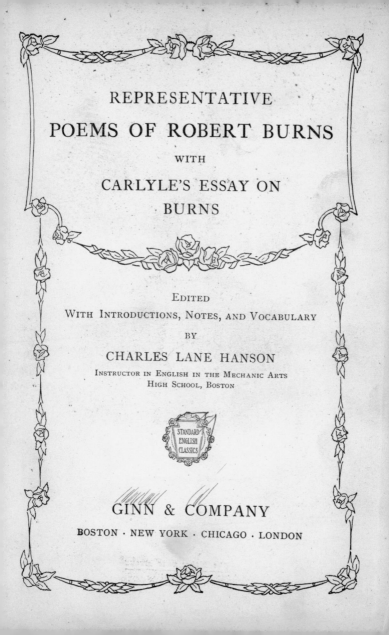

REPRESENTATIVE
POEMS OF ROBERT BURNS

WITH

CARLYLE'S ESSAY ON
BURNS

EDITED

WITH INTRODUCTIONS, NOTES, AND VOCABULARY

BY

CHARLES LANE HANSON

INSTRUCTOR IN ENGLISH IN THE MECHANIC ARTS
HIGH SCHOOL, BOSTON

STANDARD
ENGLISH
CLASSICS

GINN & COMPANY

BOSTON · NEW YORK · CHICAGO · LONDON

The Athenæum Press

GINN & COMPANY · PRO-
PRIETORS · BOSTON · U.S.A.

TO

MY BURNS SECTION

OF THE CLASS OF 1898

WORCESTER ENGLISH HIGH SCHOOL

APPRECIATIVE, SYMPATHETIC

EAGER TO LEARN

THE memory of Burns, — every man's, every boy's and girl's head carries snatches of his songs, and they say them by heart, and, what is strangest of all, never learned them from a book, but from mouth to mouth. The wind whispers them, the birds whistle them, the corn, barley, and bulrushes hoarsely rustle them, nay, the music boxes at Geneva are framed and toothed to play them; the hand organs of the Savoyards in all cities repeat them, and the chimes of bells ring them in the spires. They are the property and the solace of mankind.

RALPH WALDO EMERSON.

CONTENTS.

—•◦•—

REPRESENTATIVE POEMS.

ESSAY ON BURNS.

THE MISSION OF THE BOOK.

———◦◦———

As the poetry of Burns is his best biography, it has seemed only fair, in preparing the second edition of Carlyle's *Essay*, to introduce representative poems. In connection with the chronological arrangement, brief introductions seem necessary, and it is hoped that the few comments will stimulate thought and encourage intelligent criticism. In order that the poems may seem less formidable to those who dread the Scotch dialect, the vocabulary appears in the footnotes. After one has read the poems the short account of Burns's life may be helpful, and the reading of the poet and of his life will enable one to appreciate and enjoy Carlyle.

Phillips Brooks, in speaking of a biography, once said to the Phillips Exeter boys, "Your reading will be a live thing if you can feel the presence of your two companions, and make them, as it were, feel yours." Carlyle has introduced us to Burns so happily that there is no excuse for our not following this and another suggestion given in the same lecture : "Never lay the biography down until the man is a living, breathing, acting person. Then you may close and lose and forget the book ; the man is yours forever."

Time and again I have been surprised and delighted, after reading a tolerably good account of the poet, to find the substance of it in a form much more compact and beautiful in Carlyle's *Essay*. Carlyle's point of view is so admirable ; his criticism is so comprehensive, so fair, so sympathetic ;

his introduction of biographical material is so effective in interpreting the life and the work of Burns, that if we read it and reread it, if we absorb it, we shall soon come to know the peasant poet. The man, his life, and his work are peculiarly inseparable. Failure to recognize this has been responsible for numberless misconceptions and useless discussions of Burns. Carlyle's recognition of it and his skill in treating the three subjects as one have enabled him to make many a valuable criticism.

In the case of nearly every poem the text is that of the *Athenæum Press*, prepared by the late Professor J. G. Dow, under the general editorship of Professors G. L. Kittredge and C. T. Winchester. I have drawn freely from this scholarly edition, as well as from the more pretentious editions of William Wallace and Scott Douglas.

POEMS OF ROBERT BURNS.

———◦o◦ọ◦oo———

REPRESENTATIVE POEMS.

———

A LOVYER and a lusty bacheler,
With lokkes crulle as they were leyd in presse.
Of twenty yeer of age he was, I gesse.
Of his stature he was of evene lengthe,
And wonderly delivere and greet of strengthe;   5

. . . .

Singinge he was or floytinge, al the day;
He was as fresh as is the month of May.

. . . .

He coulde songes make and wel endite,
Juste and eek daunce and wel purtreye and write.
So hote he lovede that by nightertale   10
He sleep namore than doth a nightingale.

These lines from Chaucer's description of his squire will serve to introduce Robert Burns at the age of twenty-one. On the naturally robust frame of the vigorous lad severe toil had already left stooping shoulders, yet he 15 was attractive and full of life. The fascination of his large glowing eyes, his unusual powers of conversation, and his passion for leadership combined to make him

conspicuous in the community.   One who knew him well
could see that he was bent on becoming prominent outside of his native town.   But at the outset we notice him
merely as an impetuous young man who was continually
5 falling in love and writing verses about experiences of
which we know little.   In his twenty-third year he wrote
the following

SONG. — MARY MORISON.

O MARY, at thy window be,
  It is the wish'd, the trysted [1] hour !
10 Those smiles and glances let me see,
  That make the miser's treasure poor :
How blythely wad I bide the stoure,[2]
  A weary slave frae sun to sun,
Could I the rich reward secure,
15   The lovely Mary Morison.

Yestreen when to the trembling string [3]
  The dance gaed thro' the lighted ha',
To thee my fancy took its wing,
  I sat, but neither heard nor saw :
20 Tho' this was fair, and that was braw,[4]
  And yon the toast of a' the town,
I sigh'd, and said amang them a',
  " Ye are na Mary Morison."

O Mary, canst thou wreck his peace,
25   Wha for thy sake wad gladly die ?
Or canst thou break that heart of his,
  Whase only faut is loving thee ?

[1] agreed upon.   [2] struggle.   [3] of a village fiddler in the corner of
a barn or a schoolroom.   [4] finely dressed.

If love for love thou wilt na gie,
    At least be pity to me shown :
A thought ungentle canna be
    The thought o' Mary Morison.

This tender, quiet, beautiful lyric is the work of a singer 5
who has mastered his technic.   Some lovers of Burns will
surely agree with Hazlitt, who says : "Of all the productions of Burns, the pathetic and serious love-songs
which he has left behind him in the manner of old ballads are perhaps those which take the deepest and most 10
lasting hold of the mind.   Such are the lines to 'Mary
Morison' . . . and the song 'O my Love is like a Red,
Red Rose.'"

Buoyant as Burns was much of the time, there were
many occasions on which "fainting fits" or other symp- 15
toms more or less alarming prompted verses of such a
thoroughly serious nature as

A PRAYER

IN THE PROSPECT OF DEATH.

OH thou unknown Almighty Cause
    Of all my hope and fear !
In whose dread presence, ere an hour,   20
    Perhaps I must appear !

If I have wander'd in those paths
    Of life I ought to shun —
As something, loudly, in my breast,
    Remonstrates I have done —   25

Thou know'st that Thou hast formèd me,
    With passions wild and strong ;

> And list'ning to their witching voice
>   Has often led me wrong.
>
> Where human weakness has come short,
>   Or frailty stept aside,
> 5 Do Thou, All-good! — for such Thou art —
>   In shades of darkness hide.
>
> Where with intention I have err'd,
>   No other plea I have
> But — Thou art good; and Goodness still
> 10   Delighteth to forgive.

This plea is not unlike Whittier's thought in *The Eternal Goodness* :

> Yet in the maddening maze of things,
>   And tossed by storm and flood,
> 15 To one fixed trust my spirit clings;
>   I know that God is good!

Of a production not so remorseful nor so poetic, "A Prayer, Under the Pressure of Violent Anguish," John Stuart Blackie says: "The man who could feel and write 20 thus was not far from the best piety of the psalms of David."

In these early days we notice Burns's ability to get the point of view of dumb animals. One day Hugh Wilson, a neighbor herd boy, came anxiously running up to tell 25 Burns that the ewe had entangled herself in the tether. Burns was much amused at the alarm of the "odd, glowran, gapin' callan, about three-fourths as wise as other folk"; he set poor Mailie free, and when they returned from the plow in the evening he repeated to his brother 30 Gilbert, much as it now stands,

THE DEATH AND DYING WORDS OF POOR MAILIE,

THE AUTHOR'S ONLY PET YOWE:

An unco mournfu' Tale.

As Mailie an' her lambs thegither
Was ae day nibblin on the tether,
Upon her cloot[1] she coost[2] a hitch,[3]
An' owre[4] she warsl'd[5] in the ditch:
There, groanin, dyin, she did lie,   5
When *Hughoc* he cam doytin[6] by.

  Wi' glowrin een and lifted han's,
Poor *Hughoc* like a statue stan's;
He saw her days were near-hand ended,
But wae 's my heart! he could na mend it.   10
He gapèd wide but naething spak —
At length poor Mailie silence brak.

  "O thou, whase lamentable face
Appears to mourn my woefu' case!
My dying words attentive hear,   15
An' bear them to my Master dear.

  "Tell him, if e'er again he keep
As muckle gear[7] as buy a sheep —
Oh, bid him never tie them mair
Wi' wicked strings o' hemp or hair!   20
But ca'[8] them out to park or hill,
An' let them wander at their will:
So may his flock increase and grow
To scores o' lambs and packs o' woo'!

---

[1] hoof.   [2] cast.   [3] loop.   [4] over.   [5] struggled.   [6] walking stupidly.
[7] much wealth.   [8] drive.

" Tell him, he was a Master kin',
An' aye was guid[1] to me an' mine ;
An' now my dying charge I gie him —
My helpless lambs, I trust them wi' him.

" Oh, bid him save their harmless lives
Frae dogs, an' tods,[2] an' butchers' knives !
But gie them guid cow-milk their fill,
Till they be fit to fend[3] themsel ;
An' tent[4] them duly, e'en an' morn,
Wi' taets[5] o' hay, an' ripps[6] o' corn.

" An' may they never learn the gaets[7]
Of ither vile, wanrestfu'[8] pets,
To slink through slaps,[9] an' reave[10] an' steal
At stacks o' peas, or stocks o' kail.[11]
So may they, like their great forbears,
For monie a year come thro' the shears :
So wives will gie them bits o' bread,
An' bairns greet[12] for them when they 're dead.

" My poor toop-lamb,[13] my son an' heir,
Oh, bid him breed him up wi' care ;
An' if he live to be a beast,
To pit some havins[14] in his breast !

" An' warn him, what I winna[15] name,
To stay content wi' yowes[16] at hame ;
An' no to rin[17] an' wear his cloots,
Like ither menseless,[18] graceless brutes.

---

1 good.   2 foxes.   3 provide for.   4 take care of.   5 small quantities.
6 handfuls.   7 ways.   8 restless.   9 gaps in a fence.   10 rob.
11 cabbage.   12 weep.   13 ram.   14 sense of propriety.   15 will not.
16 ewes.   17 run.   18 indiscreet.

" And niest [1] my yowie, [2] silly thing,
Gude [3] keep thee frae a tether string !
Oh, may thou ne'er forgather [4] up
Wi' ony blastit, moorland toop,
But ay keep mind to moop [5] and mell [6]   5
Wi' sheep o' credit like thysel !

" And now, my bairns, wi' my last breath
I lea'e my blessin wi' you baith ;
And when you think upo' your mither,
Mind to be kin' to ane anither.   10

" Now, honest *Hughoc*, dinna fail
To tell my master a' my tale ;
An' bid him burn this cursed tether,
An' for thy pains thou 'se get my blether." [7]

This said, poor Mailie turn'd her head,   15
An' closed her een amang the dead !

Written later, apparently, was

POOR MAILIE'S ELEGY.

LAMENT in rhyme, lament in prose,
Wi' saut tears tricklin doun your nose ;
Our Bardie's fate is at a close,   20
    Past a' remead ; [8]
The last, sad cape-stane [9] o' his woe 's —
    Poor Mailie 's dead !

It 's no the loss o' warl's gear, [10]
    That could sae bitter draw the tear,   25

[1] next.   [2] little ewe.   [3] God.   [4] meet.   [5] nibble.   [6] associate.
[7] bladder.   [8] remedy.   [9] copestone.   [10] world's goods.

Or mak our Bardie, dowie,[1] wear
   The mournin weed :
He 's lost a friend and neebor dear,
   In Mailie dead.

5 Thro' a' the toun she trotted by him ;
A lang half-mile she could descry him ;
Wi' kindly bleat, when she did spy him,
   She ran wi' speed :
A friend mair faithfu' ne'er cam nigh him,
10   Than Mailie dead.

I wat[2] she was a sheep o' sense,
An' could behave hersel wi' mense ;[3]
I 'll say 't, she never brak a fence,
   Thro' thievish greed.
15 Our Bardie, lanely, keeps the spence[4]
   Sin Mailie 's dead.

Or, if he wanders up the howe,[5]
Her livin image in her yowe
Comes bleatin till[6] him, owre the knowe,[7]
20   For bits o' bread ;
An' down the briny pearls rowe[8]
   For Mailie dead.

She was nae get[9] o' moorlan' tips,[10]
Wi' tawted ket,[11] an' hairy hips ;
25 For her forbears were brought in ships,
   Frae yont the Tweed :
A bonier fleesh ne'er cross'd the clips[12]
   Than Mailie 's dead.

---

[1] low-spirited. [2] know. [3] decorum. [4] inner room. [5] valley. [6] to.
[7] knoll. [8] roll. [9] offspring. [10] rams. [11] matted fleece. [12] shears.

Wae worth[1] the man wha first did shape
That vile, wanchancie[2] thing — a rape !
It makes guid fellows girn an' gape,[3]
　　　　Wi' chokin dread ;
An' Robin's bonnet wave wi' crape,　　　　5
　　　　For Mailie dead.

O a' ye Bards on bonie Doon !
An' wha on Ayr your chanters[4] tune !
Come, join the melancholious croon
　　　　O' Robin's reed !　　　　10
His heart will never get aboon —[5]
　　　　His Mailie's dead.

Farming was hard work for Burns ; he preferred the
lyre to the plow.　To show which class of men he belonged
to he wrote the　　　　15

SONG, — GREEN GROW THE RASHES.

CHORUS. — GREEN grow the rashes,[6] O !
　　　　Green grow the rashes, O !
　　　　　The sweetest hours that e'er I spend
　　　　Are spent amang the lasses, O.

There 's nought but care on ev'ry han',　　　　20
　　　　In every hour that passes, O :
What signifies the life o' man,
　　　　An 't were na for the lasses, O ?

The war'ly[7] race may riches chase,
　　　　An' riches still may fly them, O ;　　　　25

---

1 woe be to.　　2 unlucky.　　3 gnash the teeth.　　4 pipes of a bagpipe.
5 above.　　6 rushes.　　7 worldly.

An' tho' at last they catch them fast,
　　Their hearts can ne'er enjoy them, O.

But gie me a cannie [1] hour at e'en,
　　My arms about my dearie, O;
An' war'ly cares, an' war'ly men,
　　May a' gae tapsalteerie,[2] O.

For you sae douce,[3] ye sneer at this;
　　Ye 're nought but senseless asses, O:
The wisest man the warl' e'er saw,
　　He dearly lov'd the lasses O.

Auld Nature swears, the lovely dears
　　Her noblest work she classes, O:
Her prentice han' she try'd on man,
　　An' then she made the lasses, O.

As these verses suggest, — he calls them the genuine
language of his heart, — he turned instinctively from
the grave, money-getting, place-seeking men to the gay
group of pleasure-lovers.　Yet the struggling peasant
poet, always impatient of inequalities of rank, was often
in the mood of

MAN WAS MADE TO MOURN.

A DIRGE.

WHEN chill November's surly blast
　　Made fields and forests bare,
One ev'ning as I wander'd forth
　　Along the banks of Ayr,

---

¹ quiet.　　² topsy-turvy.　　³ solemn.

I spied a man, whose aged step
    Seem'd weary, worn with care;
His face was furrow'd o'er with years,
    And hoary was his hair.

"Young stranger, whither wand'rest thou?"   **5**
    Began the rev'rend sage;
"Dost thirst of wealth thy step constrain,
    Or youthful pleasure's rage?
Or haply, prest with cares and woes,
    Too soon thou hast began   **10**
To wander forth, with me to mourn
    The miseries of man.

"The sun that overhangs yon moors,
    Out-spreading far and wide,
Where hundreds labour to support   **15**
    A haughty lordling's pride;—
I've seen yon weary winter-sun
    Twice forty times return;
And ev'ry time has added proofs,
    That man was made to mourn.   **20**

"O man! while in thy early years,
    How prodigal of time!
Mis-spending all thy precious hours—
    Thy glorious, youthful prime!
Alternate follies take the sway;   **25**
    Licentious passions burn;
Which tenfold force gives Nature's law
    That man was made to mourn.

"Look not alone on youthful prime,
    Or manhood's active might;   **30**

Man then is useful to his kind,
    Supported is his right :
But see him on the edge of life,
    With cares and sorrows worn,
5   Then Age and Want, oh! ill-match'd pair —
    Shew man was made to mourn.

" A few seem favourites of fate,
    In pleasure's lap carest ;
Yet, think not all the rich and great
10   Are likewise truly blest :
But, oh! what crowds in ev'ry land
    All wretched and forlorn,
Thro' weary life this lesson learn,
    That man was made to mourn.

15   " Many and sharp the num'rous ills
    Inwoven with our frame !
More pointed still we make ourselves,
    Regret, remorse, and shame !
And man, whose heaven-erected face
20   The smiles of love adorn, —
Man's inhumanity to man
    Makes countless thousands mourn !

" See yonder poor, o'erlabour'd wight,
    So abject, mean, and vile,
25   Who begs a brother of the earth
    To give him leave to toil ;
And see his lordly fellow-worm
    The poor petition spurn,
Unmindful, tho' a weeping wife
30   And helpless offspring mourn.

" If I 'm design'd yon lordling's slave,
  By Nature's law design'd,
Why was an independent wish
  E'er planted in my mind ?
If not, why am I subject to   5
  His cruelty, or scorn ?
Or why has man the will and pow'r
  To make his fellow mourn ?

"Yet, let not this too much, my son,
  Disturb thy youthful breast ;   10
This partial view of human-kind
  Is surely not the last !
The poor, oppressèd, honest man,
  Had never, sure, been born,
Had there not been some recompense   15
  To comfort those that mourn !

"O Death ! the poor man's dearest friend,[1]
  The kindest and the best !
Welcome the hour my aged limbs
  Are laid with thee at rest !   20
The great, the wealthy fear thy blow,
  From pomp and pleasure torn ;
But, oh ! a blest relief to those
  That weary-laden mourn ! "

Up to the age of twenty-five, Burns was without serious 25
aim in life.   About that time he wrote of his wish to be a
poet.   " The romantic woodlands & sequestered scenes
of Aire . . . & the winding sweep of Doon " needed a

---

[1] " A WORLD TO COME ! is the only genuine balm for an agonising heart,
torn to pieces in the wrench of parting forever (to mortal view) with friends,
inmates of the bosom and dear to the soul." — *Burns to Mrs. Dunlop, 1790.*

singer. "Alas! I am far unequal to the task, both in
native genius and education.   Obscure I am & obscure I
must be, though no young Poet nor Young Soldier's heart
ever beat more fondly for fame than mine."   A few
5 months later appeared the

SONG,—RANTIN ROVIN ROBIN.

THERE was a lad was born in Kyle,[1]
But whatna [2] day o' whatna style,[3]
I doubt it 's hardly worth the while
    To be sae nice wi' Robin.

10   CHORUS. ── Robin was a rovin boy,
                Rantin,[4] rovin, rantin, rovin;
            Robin was a rovin boy,
                Rantin, rovin Robin.

Our monarch's hindmost year but ane
15   Was five-and-twenty days begun,[5]
'T was then a blast o' Janwar' win'
    Blew hansel [6] in on Robin.

The gossip [7] keekit [8] in his loof,[9]
Quo' scho,[10] "Wha lives will see the proof,
20   This waly [11] boy will be nae coof;[12]
    I think we 'll ca' him Robin.

---

1 the central district of Ayrshire, between the Irvine and the Doon.   2 what
particular.   3 whether "old style" or "new style."   4 full of animal
spirits.   5 George II; 25 January, 1759.   6 first money, or gift,
bestowed on a special occasion.   7 sponsor in baptism.   8 peeped.
9 palm.   10 she.   11 goodly.   12 fool.

" He 'll hae misfortunes great and sma',
But aye a heart aboon them a' ;
He 'll be a credit till [1] us a' —
    We 'll a' be proud o' Robin.

" But sure as three times three mak nine,   5
I see by ilka [2] score and line,
This chap will dearly like our kin',
    So leeze [3] me on thee, Robin."

Without overestimating his ability, Burns was coura-
geous and confident. Within little more than a year he 10
wrote most of the poems that have made him famous, and
about this time he began to think of publishing.

During the autumn and winter seasons some of his best
verses were composed while he was holding the plow.
On one occasion the boy who was guiding the horses ran 15
after a field mouse to kill it with the "pattle." Burns
promptly called him back, and soon afterward read to
him the poem

TO A MOUSE,

ON TURNING UP HER NEST WITH THE PLOUGH,
NOVEMBER, 1785.

WEE, sleekit, cowrin, tim'rous beastie,
Oh, what a panic 's in thy breastie !   20
Thou need na start awa sae hasty
    Wi' bickerin brattle ! [4]
I wad be laith to rin an' chase thee
    Wi' murd'rin pattle ! [5]

---

[1] to.   [2] each, every.   [3] blessings on.   [4] hasty scamper.   [5] a spade
to remove clay that clung to the plowshare.

I 'm truly sorry man's dominion
Has broken nature's social union,
An' justifies that ill opinion
       Which makes thee startle
5   At me, thy poor earth-born companion,
       An' fellow-mortal !

I doubt na, whyles,[1] but thou may thieve :
What then ? poor beastie, thou maun live !
A daimen icker in a thrave[2]
10   'S a sma' request ;
I 'll get a blessin wi' the lave,[3]
       An' never miss 't !

Thy wee bit housie, too, in ruin !
Its silly[4] wa's[5] the win's[6] are strewin !
15   An' naething, now, to big[7] a new ane,
       O' foggage[8] green !
An' bleak December's winds ensuin
       Baith snell[9] an' keen !

Thou saw the fields laid bare and waste,
20   An' weary winter comin fast,
An' cozie here beneath the blast
       Thou thought to dwell,
Till crash ! the cruel coulter past
       Out thro' thy cell.

25   That wee bit heap o' leaves an' stibble
Has cost thee mony a weary nibble !
Now thou 's turn'd out for[10] a' thy trouble,

---

1 sometimes.   2 an occasional ear of grain in twenty-four sheaves.
   3 remainder.   4 weak.   5 walls.   6 winds.   7 build.
   8 rank grass.   9 biting.   10 in return for.

> But[1] house or hald,[2]
> To thole[3] the winter's sleety dribble
> An' cranreuch[4] cauld !

> But, Mousie, thou art no thy lane[5]
> In proving foresight may be vain :
> The best laid schemes o' mice an' men
> Gang aft a-gley,
> An' lea'e us nought but grief an' pain
> For promis'd joy.

> Still thou art blest, compar'd wi' me !
> The present only toucheth thee :
> But, och ! I backward cast my ee
> On prospects drear !
> An' forward, tho' I canna see,
> I guess an' fear !

From this expression of the poet's fine, sincere sympathy with nature we turn to a picture of family life. It becomes doubly attractive when we consider it as a faithful revelation of Scottish home life, family devotion and patriotism. And we cherish it all the more because it gives us a glimpse of Burns's own father and his home. After the father's death Burns, as the oldest son, took his place at devotions. He conducted the family worship every night when at home during his residence at Mossgiel.

[1] without.   [2] holding.   [3] endure.   [4] hoarfrost.   [5] not alone.

THE COTTER'S SATURDAY NIGHT.

INSCRIBED TO ROBERT AIKEN, ESQ.

> Let not Ambition mock their useful toil,
> Their homely joys and destiny obscure;
> Nor Grandeur hear with a disdainful smile
> The short and simple annals of the poor. — GRAY.

My lov'd, my honour'd, much respected friend!
  No mercenary bard his homage pays;
With honest pride, I scorn each selfish end:
  My dearest meed a friend's esteem and praise.
5 To you I sing, in simple Scottish lays,
  The lowly train in life's sequester'd scene;
    The native feelings strong, the guileless ways;
  What Aiken in a cottage would have been;
Ah! tho' his worth unknown, far happier there, I ween!

10 November chill blaws loud wi' angry sugh,
  The short'ning winter day is near a close;
The miry beasts retreating frae the pleugh,
  The black'ning trains o' craws to their repose;
  The toil-worn Cotter frae his labour goes, —
15 This night his weekly moil[1] is at an end, —
  Collects his spades, his mattocks, and his hoes,
Hoping the morn in ease and rest to spend,
And weary, o'er the moor, his course does hameward bend.

At length his lonely cot appears in view,
20 Beneath the shelter of an agèd tree;
Th' expectant wee-things, toddlin, stacher[2] through
  To meet their dad, wi' flichterin[3] noise an' glee.
His wee bit ingle,[4] blinkin bonilie,

---

[1] toil.   [2] stagger.   [3] fluttering.   [4] fireplace.

His clean hearth-stane, his thrifty wifie's smile,
　　The lisping infant prattling on his knee,
Does a' his weary kiaugh [1] and care [2] beguile,
An' makes him quite forget his labour an' his toil.

Belyve, [3] the elder bairns come drappin in,　　　　　　　　5
　　At service out amang the farmers roun';
Some ca the pleugh, some herd, some tentie [4] rin
　　A cannie [5] errand to a neibor toun: [6]
　　Their eldest hope, their Jenny, woman-grown,
In youthfu' bloom, love sparkling in her ee,　　　　　　　10
　　Comes hame, perhaps to shew a braw new gown,
Or deposit her sair-won penny-fee,
To help her parents dear, if they in hardship be.

With joy unfeign'd brothers and sisters meet,
　　An' each for other's weelfare kindly spiers: [7]　　　　15
The social hours, swift-wing'd, unnotic'd fleet;
　　Each tells the uncos [8] that he sees or hears.
　　The parents, partial, eye their hopeful years;
Anticipation forward points the view;
　　The mother, wi' her needle an' her sheers,　　　　　　20
Gars [9] auld claes look amaist as weel 's the new;
The father mixes a' wi' admonition due.

Their master's an' their mistress's command
　　The younkers a' are warned to obey;
An' mind their labours wi' an eydent [10] hand,　　　　　25
　　An' ne'er, tho' out o' sight, to jauk [11] or play:
　　"An' O! be sure to fear the Lord alway,

---

[1] fret.　　[2] the original words, changed in a later edition to "carking cares."
　　[3] presently.　　[4] attentive.　　[5] careful.　　[6] farm.　　[7] asks.
　　[8] news.　　[9] makes.　　[10] diligent.　　[11] trifle.

An' mind your duty, duly, morn an' night !
 Lest in temptation's path ye gang astray,
Implore His counsel and assisting might :
They never sought in vain that sought the Lord aright ! "

5 But hark ! a rap comes gently to the door.
 Jenny, wha kens the meaning o' the same,
Tells how a neibor lad cam o'er the moor,
 To do some errands, and convoy her hame.
 The wily mother sees the conscious flame
10 Sparkle in Jenny's ee, and flush her cheek ;
 Wi' heart-struck, anxious care, inquires his name,
While Jenny hafflins [1] is afraid to speak ;
Weel pleas'd the mother hears it's nae wild worthless rake.

Wi' kindly welcome Jenny brings him ben,[2]
15 A strappin youth ; he takes the mother's eye ;
Blythe Jenny sees the visit's no ill taen ;
 The father cracks [3] of horses, pleughs, and kye.
 The youngster's artless heart o'erflows wi' joy,
But, blate [4] and laithfu',[5] scarce can weel behave ;
20 The mother wi' a woman's wiles [6] can spy
What maks the youth sae bashfu' an' sae grave,
Weel pleas'd to think her bairn's respected like the lave.[7]

O happy love ! where love like this is found !
 O heart-felt raptures ! bliss beyond compare !
25 I've pacèd much this weary, mortal round,
 And sage experience bids me this declare —
 "If Heaven a draught of heavenly pleasure spare,
One cordial in this melancholy vale,
 'T is when a youthful, loving, modest pair,
30 In other's arms breathe out the tender tale,
Beneath the milk-white thorn that scents the ev'ning gale."

[1] partly. [2] in. [3] talks. [4] bashful. [5] shy. [6] penetration. [7] rest.

Is there, in human form, that bears a heart,
    A wretch! a villain! lost to love and truth!
That can with studied, sly, ensnaring art
    Betray sweet Jenny's unsuspecting youth?
    Curse on his perjur'd arts! dissembling smooth!   5
Are honour, virtue, conscience, all exil'd?
    Is there no pity, no relenting ruth,
Points to the parents fondling o'er their child,
Then paints the ruin'd maid, and their distraction wild?

But now the supper crowns their simple board,   10
    The halesome parritch,[1] chief of Scotia's food;
The sowpe[2] their only hawkie[3] does afford,
    That yont the hallan[4] snugly chows her cud.
    The dame brings forth, in complimental mood,
To grace the lad, her weel-hain'd kebbuck[5] fell,   15
    An' aft[6] he's prest, an' aft he ca's it guid;[7]
The frugal wifie, garrulous, will tell,
How 't was a towmond[8] auld, sin' lint was i' the bell.[9]

The cheerfu' supper done, wi' serious face,
    They round the ingle form a circle wide;   20
The sire turns o'er with patriarchal grace
    The big ha'-bible,[10] ance his father's pride;
    His bonnet rev'rently is laid aside,
His lyart haffets[11] wearing thin and bare;
    Those strains that once did sweet in Zion glide,   25
He wales[12] a portion with judicious care;
And, "Let us worship GOD," he says with solemn air.

They chant their artless notes in simple guise;
    They tune their hearts, by far the noblest aim:

---

[1] porridge.   [2] liquid food.   [3] cow.   [4] porch.   [5] well-spared cheese.
[6] often.   [7] good.   [8] twelvemonth.   [9] flax in flower.   [10] large family
Bible kept in the hall or chief room.   [11] gray side-locks.   [12] selects.

Perhaps *Dundee's*[1] wild-warbling measures rise,
　　Or plaintive *Martyrs*,[1] worthy of the name,
　　Or noble *Elgin*[1] beets[2] the heaven-ward flame,
The sweetest far of Scotia's holy lays.
5　　　Compar'd with these, Italian trills are tame;
　　The tickl'd ear no heart-felt raptures raise;
Nae unison hae they with our Creator's praise.

The priest-like father reads the sacred page, —
　　How Abram was the friend of GOD on high;
10　Or Moses bade eternal warfare wage
　　With Amalek's ungracious progeny;
　　Or how the royal bard did groaning lie
Beneath the stroke of heaven's avenging ire;
　　Or Job's pathetic plaint, and wailing cry;
15　Or rapt Isaiah's wild, seraphic fire;
Or other holy seers that tune the sacred lyre.

Perhaps the Christian volume is the theme, —
　　How guiltless blood for guilty man was shed;
How HE, who bore in heav'n the second name,
20　　Had not on earth whereon to lay His head:
　　How His first followers and servants sped;[3]
The precepts sage they wrote to many a land:[4]
　　How he, who lone in Patmos banishèd,
　　Saw in the sun a mighty angel stand,
25 And heard great Bab'lon's doom pronounced by Heav'n's
　　　　command.[5]

Then kneeling down to HEAVEN'S ETERNAL KING,
　　The saint, the father, and the husband prays:
Hope " springs exulting on triumphant wing,"

---

[1] favorite psalm tunes.　　　[2] adds fuel to.　　　[3] the Acts of the Apostles.
　　　　　[4] the Epistles.　　　[5] the Apocalypse.

That thus they all shall meet in future days :
  There ever bask in uncreated rays,
No more to sigh or shed the bitter tear,
  Together hymning their Creator's praise,
In such society, yet still more dear,   5
While circling Time moves round in an eternal sphere.

Compar'd with this, how poor Religion's pride
  In all the pomp of method and of art,
When men display to congregations wide
  Devotion's ev'ry grace except the heart !   10
  The Pow'r, incens'd, the pageant will desert,
The pompous strain, the sacerdotal stole ;
  But haply in some cottage far apart
May hear, well pleased, the language of the soul,
And in His book of life the inmates poor enrol.   15

Then homeward all take off their sev'ral way ;
  The youngling cottagers retire to rest ;
The parent-pair their secret homage pay,
  And proffer up to Heav'n the warm request,
  That He, who stills the raven's clam'rous nest   20
And decks the lily fair in flow'ry pride,
  Would, in the way His wisdom sees the best,
For them and for their little ones provide ;
But chiefly, in their hearts with grace divine preside.

From scenes like these old Scotia's grandeur springs,   25
  That makes her lov'd at home, rever'd abroad :
Princes and lords are but the breath of kings,
  " An honest man 's the noblest work of God " :[1]

[1] *Cf.* Fletcher's

> Man is his own star ; and that soul that can
> Be honest is the only perfect man,

and Pope, *Essay on Man*, 247.

And certes, in fair Virtue's heavenly road,
The cottage leaves the palace far behind :
    What is a lordling's pomp ? a cumbrous load,
Disguising oft the wretch of human kind,
5 Studied in arts of hell, in wickedness refin'd !

O Scotia ! my dear, my native soil !
    For whom my warmest wish to Heaven is sent !
Long may thy hardy sons of rustic toil
    Be blest with health, and peace, and sweet content !
10   And, oh ! may Heaven their simple lives prevent
From luxury's contagion, weak and vile !
    Then, howe'er crowns and coronets be rent,
A virtuous populace may rise the while,
And stand a wall of fire around their much-lov'd isle.

15   O Thou ! who pour'd the patriotic tide
    That stream'd thro' Wallace's[1] undaunted heart,
Who dar'd to nobly stem tyrannic pride,
    Or nobly die, the second glorious part, —
    (The patriot's God peculiarly thou art,
20   His friend, inspirer, guardian, and reward !)
    O never, never Scotia's realm desert,
But still the patriot, and the patriot-bard,
In bright succession raise, her ornament and guard !

In this triumph of piety and morality over poverty
25 Burns gives us a part of his philosophy of life. Like
Goldsmith, he believes that happiness depends not on
wealth or rank, but on the heart. In the *Epistle to Davie*
he says :

    If happiness hae not her seat
30   And centre in the breast,

---

1 the outlaw knight, William Wallace, who in 1297 roused the Scots to
demand their freedom ; the national hero.

We may be wise, or rich, or great,
    But never can be blest:
      Nae treasures, nor pleasures,
        Could make us happy lang;
      The heart ay 's the part ay,   5
        That makes us right or wrang.

Sainte-Beuve says that in this poem Burns is not only picturesque but "cordial, moral, Christian, patriotic. His episode of Jenny introduces and personifies the chastity of emotion; the Bible, read aloud, casts a religious glow 10 over the whole scene. Then come those lofty thoughts upon the greatness of old Scotland, which is based on such home scenes as this."

Burns included in his family the faithful companion whom he introduces in the poem 15

THE AULD FARMER'S NEW-YEAR MORNING SAL-
UTATION TO HIS AULD MARE, MAGGIE,

ON GIVING HER THE ACCUSTOMED RIPP OF CORN TO HANSEL
IN THE NEW YEAR.

A GUID New-Year I wish thee, Maggie!
Hae, there 's a ripp[1] to thy auld baggie:[2]
Tho' thou 's howe-backit[3] now, an' knaggie,[4]
    I 've seen the day
Thou could hae gane like ony staggie[5]   20
    Out-owre the lay.[6]

Tho' now thou 's dowie,[7] stiff, an' crazy,
An' thy auld hide 's as white 's a daisie,
I 've seen thee dappl't, sleek an' glaizie,[8]

---

[1] handful.   [2] stomach.   [3] hollow-backed.   [4] bony.   [5] colt.   [6] lea.
[7] low-spirited.   [8] glossy.

A bonie gray :
He should been tight that daur't to raize thee,[1]
            Ance in a day.

Thou ance was i' the foremost rank,
5   A filly buirdly,[2] steeve,[3] an' swank,[4]
An' set weel down a shapely shank
            As e'er tread yird ;[5]
An' could hae flown out-owre a stank[6]
            Like ony bird.

10   It's now some nine-and-twenty year
Sin' thou was my guid-father's meere ;[7]
He gied me thee, o' tocher[8] clear,
            An' fifty mark ;
Tho' it was sma', 't was weel won gear,[9]
15   An' thou was stark.[10]

When first I gaed to woo my Jenny,
Ye then was trottin wi' your minnie :[11]
Tho' ye was trickie, slee and funny,
            Ye ne'er was donsie ;[12]
20   But hamely, tawie,[13] quiet an' cannie,[14]
            An' unco sonsie.[15]

That day ye pranc'd wi' mickle pride,
When ye bure hame my bonie bride :
An' sweet an' gracefu' she did ride,
25   Wi' maiden air !
Kyle-Stewart I could braggèd wide[16]
            For sic a pair.

---

[1] He should have been girt for action that dared to excite thee.   [2] strong.
[3] firm.   [4] stately.   [5] earth.   [6] ditch.   [7] father-in-law's mare.
[8] dowry.   [9] well-earned money.   [10] strong.   [11] mother.   [12] mis-
chievous.   [13] tame.   [14] safe.   [15] very plump.   [16] I could
have challenged the country between the Irvine and the Ayr.

Tho' now ye dow[1] but hoyte an' hoble[2]
An' wintle[3] like a saumont-coble,[4]
That day ye was a jinker[5] noble
    For heels an' win'![6]
An' ran them till they a' did wauble[7]   5
    Far, far behin'!

When thou an' I were young an' skiegh,[8]
An' stable meals at fairs were driegh,[9]
How thou wad prance an' snore an' skriegh[10]
    An' tak' the road!   10
Toun's bodies ran an' stood abiegh[11]
    An' ca't[12] thee mad.

When thou was corn't an' I was mellow,
We took the road ay like a swallow:
At brooses[13] thou had ne'er a fellow   15
    For pith an' speed;
But ev'ry tail thou pay't them hollow,
    Whare'er thou gaed.

The sma', droop-rumpl't,[14] hunter cattle
Might aiblins[15] waur't[16] thee for a brattle;[17]   20
But sax[18] Scotch mile thou try't their mettle
    An' gart[19] them whaizle:[20]
Nae whip nor spur, but just a wattle[21]
    O' saugh[22] or hazel.

Thou was a noble fittie-lan'[23]   25
As e'er in tug or tow[24] was drawn!

---

[1] can.   [2] limp.   [3] stagger.   [4] salmon-boat.   [5] runner.   [6] wind.
[7] reel.   [8] high-mettled.   [9] tedious.   [10] whinny.   [11] out of the way.   [12] called.   [13] A *broose* is a race at a country wedding.
[14] drooping at the crupper.   [15] perhaps.   [16] beat.   [17] spurt.
[18] six.   [19] made.   [20] wheeze.   [21] switch.   [22] willow.
[23] foot-the-land; the near horse of the hinder pair in plowing, which does not step in the furrow.   [24] rope.

Aft thee an' I, in aught hours' gaun [1]
   On guid March-weather,
Hae turn'd sax rood [2] beside our han'
   For days thegither.

5 Thou never braing't [3] an' fetch't [4] an' flisket, [5]
But thy auld tail thou wad hae whisket [6]
An' spread abreed thy weel-fill'd brisket, [7]
   Wi' pith an' pow'r,
Till spritty knowes wad rair't and risket
10   An' slypet owre. [8]

When frosts lay lang an' snaws were deep
An' threaten'd labour back to keep,
I gied thy cog a wee-bit heap
   Aboon the timmer : [9]
15 I ken'd my Maggie wad na sleep
   For that, [10] or simmer. [11]

In cart or car thou never reestet ;
The steyest brae [12] thou wad hae faced it ;
Thou never lap [13] an' sten't an' breastet, [14]
20   Then stood to blaw ;
But just thy step a wee thing hastet,
   Thou snoov 't awa. [15]

My pleugh is now thy bairn-time a', [16]
Four gallant brutes as e'er did draw ;
25 Forbye [17] sax mae [18] I 've sell 't awa,

---

1 eight hours' going. 2 six roods. 3 fretted. 4 raged. 5 kicked.
6 lashed. 7 breast. 8 "Till hillocks, where the earth was full of
tough-rooted plants, would have given forth a cracking sound, and the
clods fallen gently over." — *Shairp.* 9 filled thy measure of oats to
overflowing. 10 "On account of the late season" the spring work
would be harder. 11 before summer. 12 steepest hill. 13 leaped.
14 reared. 15 moved on steadily. 16 My plowing team of four
horses are now thine offspring. 17 besides. 18 six more.

That thou hast nurst:
They drew me thretteen[1] pund an' twa,
The vera warst.

Mony a sair daurg[2] we twa hae wrought,
An' wi' the weary warl' fought!   5
An' mony an anxious day I thought
  We wad be beat!
Yet here to crazy age we 're brought
  Wi' something yet.

And think na, my auld trusty servan', 10
That now, perhaps, thou 's less deservin,
And thy auld days may end in stervin;
  For my last fou,[3]
A heapit stimpart,[4] I 'll reserve ane,
  Laid by for you.   15

We 've worn to crazy years thegither;
We 'll toyte[5] about wi' ane anither;
Wi' tentie[6] care I 'll flit thy tether
  To some hained rig,[7]
Whare ye may noble rax[8] your leather, 20
  Wi' sma' fatigue.

Dow says this is " the *John Anderson, my jo*, of Burns's poems. It portrays a long and tried friendship and those relations of human intimacy that are common between the country people of Scotland and their domestic animals." 25

Know Burns, know his dog. We are quite ready to make the acquaintance of a favorite dog, Luath. In order to give Luath an opportunity to speak for himself the poet created an imaginary Cæsar.

---

[1] thirteen. [2] heavy day's work. [3] measure of grain. [4] quarter of a peck.
[5] totter. [6] heedful. [7] reserved piece of ground. [8] stretch.

THE TWA DOGS.

A TALE.

'T was in that place o' Scotland's isle,
That bears the name o' auld King Coil,[2]
Upon a bonie day in June,
When wearin' through the afternoon,
5   Twa dogs that werena thrang[2] at hame
Forgathered ance upon a time.

   The first I 'll name, they ca'd him Cæsar,
Was keepit for his Honour's pleasure;
His hair, his size, his mouth, his lugs,[3]
10   Showed he was nane o' Scotland's dogs;
But whalpit[4] some place far abroad,
Whare sailors gang to fish for cod.[5]

   His lockèd, letter'd, braw brass collar
Show'd him the gentleman and scholar;
15   But though he was o' high degree,
The fient a pride[6] — nae pride had he;[7]
But wad hae spent an hour caressin,
Even wi' a tinkler-gypsy's messan :[8]
At kirk or market, mill or smiddie,[9]
20   Nae tawted tyke,[10] though e'er sae duddie,[11]
But he wad stan't,[12] as glad to see him,
And stroan't on stanes[13] and hillocks wi' him.

---

1 Kyle; cf. *Rantin Rovin Robin*, 1.   Tradition says the district derived its
name from Coilus, "king of the Picts."   2 busy.   3 ears.   4 whelped.
5 Newfoundland.   6 no pride whatever.   7 Cf. *Lines on an Interview with Lord Daer*.   8 vagabond-gypsy's cur.   9 smithy.
10 matted dog.   11 unkempt.   12 have stood.   13 stones.

The tither was a ploughman's collie,
A rhymin, rantin, ravin billie,[1]
Wha for his friend and comrade had him,
An' in his freaks had Luath ca'd him,
After some dog in Highland sang,[2]   5
Was made lang syne, — Lord knows how lang.

He was a gash[3] an' faithfu' tyke,
As ever lap[4] a sheugh[5] or dike.[6]
His honest, sonsie,[7] baws'nt face[8]
Ay gat him friends in ilka place;   10
His breast was white, his touzie[9] back
Weel clad wi' coat o' glossy black;
His gawcie[10] tail wi' upward curl
Hung owre his hurdies[11] wi' a swirl.

Nae doubt but they were fain[12] o' ither,   15
An' unco pack an' thick thegither;
Wi' social nose whyles[13] snuff'd[14] and snowket;
Whyles mice and moudieworts[15] they howket;[16]
Whyles scour'd awa in lang excursion
An' worry'd ither in diversion;[17]   20
Until wi' daffin weary grown,
Upon a knowe[18] they sat them down,
An' there began a lang digression
About the 'lords o' the creation.'

CÆSAR.

I 've aften wondered, honest Luath,   25
What sort o' life poor dogs like you have;

---

[1] fellow.   [2] Cuchullin's dog in Ossian's *Fingal.—B.*   [3] wise.   [4] leaped.
[5] ditch.   [6] wall.   [7] handsome.   [8] with a white stripe down the
face.   [9] shaggy.   [10] big and lusty.   [11] hips.   [12] fond.
[13] sometimes.   [14] scented.   [15] moles.   [16] dug up.   [17] romping.
[18] knoll.

And when the gentry's life I saw,
What way poor bodies liv'd ava.[1]

Our laird gets in his racket rents,
His coals, his kain,[2] and a' his stents;[3]
5   He rises when he likes himsel;
His flunkies answer at the bell;
He ca's his coach, he ca's his horse;
He draws a bonie silken purse
As lang 's my tail, where through the steeks[4]
10 The yellow-lettered Geordie keeks.[5]

Frae morn to e'en it 's nought but toilin,
At bakin, roastin, fryin, boilin;
And though the gentry first are stechin,[6]
Yet ev'n the ha'-folk[7] fill their pechan[8]
15 Wi' sauce, ragouts, an' sic like trashtrie,
That 's little short o' downright wastrie.
Our whipper-in, wee blastit wonner,[9]
Poor worthless elf, it eats a dinner
Better than ony tenant man
20 His Honour has in a' the lan';
And what poor cot-folk pit[10] their painch[11] in,
I own it 's past my comprehension.

LUATH.

Trowth, Cæsar, whiles they 're fash't[12] eneugh;
A cotter howkin[13] in a sheugh,[14]
25 Wi' dirty stanes biggin[15] a dyke,[16]
Barin a quarry, and sic like;

---

[1] at all.   [2] farm produce paid as rent.   [3] taxes.   [4] stitches.   [5] guinea
peeps.   [6] stuffing.   [7] kitchen people.   [8] belly.   [9] shrivelled-up
wonder.   [10] put.   [11] stomach.   [12] troubled.   [13] digging.
[14] ditch.   [15] building.   [16] wall.

Himsel, a wife, he thus sustains,
A smytrie o' wee duddie weans,[1]
And nought but his han'-daurg[2] to keep
Them right and tight in thack and rape.[3]

And when they meet wi' sair disasters,   5
Like loss o' health or want o' masters,
Ye maist wad think, a wee touch langer,
And they maun starve o' cauld and hunger;
But how it comes, I never kenn'd yet,
They 're maistly wonderfu' contented: 10
And buirdly chiels[4] an' clever hizzies[5]
Are bred in sic a way as this is.

CÆSAR.

But then to see how you 're neglecket,
How huff'd and cuff'd and disrespecket!
Lord, man, our gentry care as little   15
For delvers, ditchers and sic cattle;
They gang as saucy by poor folk,
As I wad by a stinkin brock.[6]

I 've noticed, on our Laird's court-day, —[7]
And mony a time my heart 's been wae, —   20
Poor tenant bodies, scant o' cash,
How they maun thole[8] a factor's snash:[9]
He 'll stamp and threaten, curse, and swear
He 'll apprehend them, poind[10] their gear;[11]

---

[1] a number of little ragged children. [2] single-handed day's labor. [3] thatch
and rope to bind it, *i.e.*, "the necessaries of life." [4] stalwart men.
[5] women. [6] badger. [7] The factor is the landlord's agent, to whom
on court-day the tenants pay their rent. [8] endure. [9] abuse.
[10] impound. [11] goods.

While they maun stan' wi' aspect humble,
And hear it a', and fear and tremble !

I see how folk live that hae riches;
But surely poor folk maun be wretches !

LUATH.

5   They 're no sae wretched 's ane wad think :
Tho' constantly on poortith's [1] brink,
They 're sae accustom'd wi' the sight,
The view o 't gies them little fright.

    Then chance and fortune are sae guided,
10   They 're aye in less or mair provided;
And tho' fatigu'd wi' close employment,
A blink o' rest 's a sweet enjoyment.

    The dearest comfort o' their lives,
Their grushie weans [2] and faithfu' wives;
15   The prattling things are just their pride,
That sweetens a' their fireside.

    And whiles twalpennie worth o' nappy [3]
Can mak the bodies unco [4] happy :
They lay aside their private cares,
20   To mind the Kirk and State affairs ;
They 'll talk o' patronage an' priests,
Wi' kindling fury i' their breasts,
Or tell what new taxation 's comin,
An' ferlie [5] at the folk in Lon'on.

25   As bleak-fac'd Hallowmas returns,
They get the jovial, ranting kirns, [6]

---

[1] poverty.   [2] thriving children.   [3] ale.   [4] very.   [5] wonder.
[6] the merry harvest-home rejoicings; rustic feasts.

When rural life o' ev'ry station
Unite in common recreation;
Love blinks, Wit slaps,[1] an' social Mirth
Forgets there 's Care upo' the earth.

That merry day the year begins,　　　　　　5
They bar the door on frosty winds;
The nappy reeks[2] wi' mantlin ream[3]
An' sheds a heart-inspirin steam;
The luntin[4] pipe an' sneeshin mill[5]
Are handed round wi' right guid will;　　　10
The cantie[6] auld folks crackin crouse,[7]
The young anes rantin[8] thro' the house, —
My heart has been sae fain to see them,
That I for joy hae barket wi' them.

Still it 's owre true that ye hae said,　　　15
Sic game is now owre aften play'd.
There 's monie a creditable stock
O' decent, honest, fawsont[9] folk
Are riven[10] out baith root an' branch,
Some rascal's pridefu' greed to quench,　　　20
Wha thinks to knit himsel the faster
In favour wi' some gentle master,[11]
Wha, aiblins thrang a-parliamentin,[12]
For Britain's guid his saul[13] indentin —

CÆSAR.

Haith,[14] lad, ye little ken about it;　　　25
For Britain's guid! guid faith! I doubt it.

---

[1] shines forth.　[2] ale smokes.　[3] froth.　[4] smoking.　[5] snuffbox.　[6] cheery.
[7] talking briskly.　[8] frolicking.　[9] seemly.　[10] torn.　[11] master of
gentle birth; the laird. The rascal is the factor.　[12] perhaps busy in
Parliament.　[13] soul.　[14] faith.

Say rather, gaun[1] as Premiers lead him,
An' saying *ay* or *no* 's they bid him :
At operas an' plays parading,
Mortgaging, gambling, masquerading :
5   Or maybe, in a frolic daft,[2]
To Hague or Calais taks a waft,
To mak a tour an' tak a whirl
To learn *bon ton* an' see the worl'.

There, at Vienna or Versailles,
10   He rives his father's auld entails ;[3]
Or by Madrid he taks the rout[4]
To thrum guitars an' fecht[5] wi' nowt ;[6]
Or down Italian vista startles,
Whore-hunting amang groves o' myrtles ;
15   Then bouses drumly[7] German-water,
To mak himsel look fair and fatter,
And clear the consequential sorrows,
Love-gifts of Carnival signoras.

For Britain's guid ! — for her destruction !
20   Wi' dissipation, feud, and faction.

LUATH.

Hech man ! dear sirs ! is that the gate[8]
They waste sae mony a braw[9] estate ?
Are we sae foughten[10] and harass'd
For gear[11] to gang that gate[12] at last ?

---

[1] going.   [2] mad.   [3] Entailed real estate in Britain must pass to the next
male heir. An entail can be broken by an act of Parliament. Burns
here refers, says Wallace, to an extravagant heir who would rive (literally "tear") the entail so that he might burden the estate with debt.
[4] road.   [5] fight.   [6] bullocks. The word "nowt" [cattle, neat] takes
all the romance from bull-fighting. — *Dow.*   [7] drinks muddy.   [8] style.
[9] fine.   [10] troubled.   [11] wealth.   [12] road.

O would they stay aback frae courts
An' please themsels wi' countra sports,
It wad for ev'ry ane be better,
The Laird, the Tenant, an' the Cotter!
For thae frank, rantin, ramblin billies,   5
Fient haet [1] o' them 's ill-hearted fellows:
Except for breakin o' their timmer,[2]
Or speakin lightly o' their limmer,[3]
Or shootin o' a hare or moor-cock,
The ne'er-a-bit they 're ill to poor folk.   10

But will ye tell me, Master Cæsar,
Sure great folk's life 's a life o' pleasure?
Nae cauld nor hunger e'er can steer [4] them,
The vera thought o 't need na fear them.

CÆSAR.

Lord, man, were ye but whyles whare I am,   15
The gentles ye wad ne'er envy 'em.

It 's true, they need na starve or sweat
Thro' winter's cauld or simmer's heat;
They 've nae sair wark to craze their banes,
An' fill auld age wi' grips an' granes:[5]   20
But human bodies are sic fools,
For a' their colleges and schools,
That when nae real ills perplex them,
They mak enow themselves to vex them;
An' ay the less they hae to sturt [6] them,   25
In like proportion less will hurt them.

A country fellow at the pleugh,
His acres till'd, he 's right eneugh;

---

[1] not a bit.   [2] cutting down their timber.   [3] hussy.   [4] bother.
[5] groans.   [6] trouble.

A country girl at her wheel,
Her dizzens[1] done, she 's unco weel:
But gentlemen, an' ladies warst,
Wi' ev'n down want o' wark are curst.
5   They loiter, loungin, lank, an' lazy;
Tho' deil-haet[2] ails them, yet uneasy:
Their days insipid, dull, an' tasteless;
Their nights unquiet, lang, an' restless;

An' ev'n their sports, their balls an' races,
10   Their galloping thro' public places, —
There 's sic parade, sic pomp, an' art,
The joy can scarcely reach the heart.

The men cast out in party-matches,[3]
Then sowther[4] a' in deep debauches.
15   Ae night, they 're mad wi' drink an' whoring,
Niest[5] day their life is past enduring.

The Ladies arm-in-arm in clusters,
As great an' gracious a' as sisters;
But hear their absent thoughts o' ither,
20   They 're a' run deils an' jads[6] thegither.
Whiles,[7] o'er the wee bit cup and platie,
They sip the scandal-potion pretty;
Or lee-lang[8] nights, wi' crabbet[9] leuks,
Pore owre the devil's pictur'd beuks;[10]
25   Stake on a chance a farmer's stackyard,[11]
And cheat like ony unhang'd blackguard.

There 's some exceptions, man an' woman;
But this is gentry's life in common.

---

1 "dozens" of hanks of thread to be wound for weaving. — *Dow.*   2 nothing.
3 quarrel.   4 reconcile.   5 next.   6 downright devils and wicked
women.   7 sometimes.   8 livelong.   9 sour.   10 cards.   11 *I.e.,* **the
value of a whole year's crop.** — *Dow.*

By this, the sun was out o' sight,
And darker gloaming brought the night :
The bum-clock [1] humm'd wi' lazy drone ; [2]
The kye [3] stood rowtin [4] i' the loan ; [5]
When up they gat, and shook their lugs, [6]   5
Rejoic'd they were na *men* but *dogs ;*
And each took aff his several way,
Resolv'd to meet some ither day.

Cæsar gave the cotter's dog considerable enlightening information — enough, one would think, to satisfy him that the cotter's lot was by no means to be despised ; but, real dogs as they are, they go off rejoicing that they are not men.

That Burns gets the point of view of man, beast, or demon ; that his sympathy is boundless, is most pointedly suggested by these lines to the deil :

> But fare you weel, auld Nickie-ben !
> O wad ye tak a thought an' men' !
> Ye aiblins might — I dinna ken —
>   Still hae a stake :   20
> I 'm wae to think upo' yon den,
>   Ev'n for your sake !

In 1786 Burns contracted with Jean Armour a marriage which, though irregular, he considered legal ; but her parents, who would not listen to the union, did all they could to keep husband and wife apart. Burns felt disgraced ; it was a critical period ; painfully conscious of his faults, yet keenly alive to his temptations, he felt the need of pleading his own cause in an

---

[1] beetle.   [2] " The beetle wheels his droning flight " in Gray's *Elegy.*
[3] cows.   [4] lowing.   [5] ' Loan ' means here an opening between fields ot corn near, or leading to, the homestead, where cows are milked. — *Wallace.*
[6] ears.

ADDRESS TO THE UNCO GUID, OR THE RIGIDLY RIGHTEOUS.

> My son, these maxims make a rule,
>   And lump them aye thegither;
> The RIGID RIGHTEOUS is a fool,
>   The RIGID WISE anither:
> The cleanest corn that e'er was dight,[1]
>   May hae some pyles o' caff in;[2]
> So ne'er a fellow-creature slight
>   For random fits o' daffin.[3] — SOLOMON, Eccles. vii, 16.

O YE wha are sae guid yoursel,
    Sae pious and sae holy,
Ye 've nought to do but mark and tell
    Your neibour's fauts and folly!
5   Whase life is like a well-gaun mill,
    Supply'd wi' store o' water,
The heapet happer's[4] ebbing still,
    And still the clap plays clatter, —

Here me, ye venerable core,[5]
10   As counsel for poor mortals,
That frequent pass douce[6] Wisdom's door
    For glaiket[7] Folly's portals;
I for their thoughtless, careless sakes
    Would here propone defences —
15   Their donsie[8] tricks, their black mistakes,
    Their failings and mischances.

Ye see your state wi' theirs compar'd,
    And shudder at the niffer;[9]
But cast a moment's fair regard,
20   What maks the mighty differ?

[1] thrashed.   [2] grains of chaff.   [3] merriment, folly.   [4] hopper.   [5] folk.
[6] grave.   [7] giddy.   [8] wicked.   [9] exchange.

Discount what scant occasion gave,
    That purity ye pride in,
And (what's aft mair than a' the lave [1])
    Your better art o' hidin.

Think, when your castigated pulse   5
    Gies now and then a wallop, [2]
What ragings must his veins convulse
    That still eternal gallop:
Wi' wind and tide fair i' your tail,
    Right on ye scud your sea-way;   10
But in the teeth o' baith to sail,
    It maks an unco [3] leeway.

See Social Life and Glee sit down,
    All joyous and unthinking,
Till, quite transmugrify'd, they 're grown   15
    Debauchery and Drinking:
O would they stay to calculate
    Th' eternal consequences;
Or — your more dreaded hell to state —
    Damnation of expenses!   20

Ye high, exalted, virtuous Dames,
    Tied up in godly laces,
Before you gie poor Frailty names,
    Suppose a change o' cases:
A dear lov'd lad, convenience snug,   25
    A treacherous inclination —
But, let me whisper i' your lug, [4]
    Ye 're aiblins [5] nae temptation.

Then gently scan your brother man,
    Still gentler sister woman;   30

---

[1] rest.   [2] quick, agitated movement.   [3] unusual.   [4] ear.   [5] perhaps.

Tho' they may gang a kennin[1] wrang,
   To step aside is human :
One point must still be greatly dark,
   The moving *Why* they do it;
5   And just as lamely can ye mark,
   How far perhaps they rue it.

Who made the heart, 't is He alone
   Decidedly can try us,
He knows each chord, its various tone,
10   Each spring, its various bias :
Then at the balance, let 's be mute,
   We never can adjust it ;
What 's *done* we partly can compute,
   But know not what 's *resisted*.

15   Has he not stated the case so well that we do not need
to speak in his behalf ?

   Those of us who are in the habit of thinking we are
"unco guid" may well consider that we are somewhat
"indebted to the world's good opinion because the world
20 does not know all."   Robert Louis Stevenson, whose plain
statements of disagreeable truths about Burns never suggest that he is winking at weaknesses, says : " Alas ! I
fear every man and woman of us is 'greatly dark' to all
their neighbours, from the day of birth until death re-
25 moves them, in their greatest virtues as well as in their
saddest faults ; and we, who have been trying to read the
character of Burns, may take home the lesson and be
gentle in our thoughts."

   Ewe, mare, dog and field-mouse had in turn been cele-
30 brated by the poet.   That he should recognize the louse as

---

[1] a little bit.

a fit subject for verse has distressed some persons, but one
needs the entire poem in order to appreciate the immortal
last stanza.

TO A LOUSE.

ON SEEING ONE ON A LADY'S BONNET AT CHURCH.

HA! whaur ye gaun, ye crowlin' ferlie![1]
Your impudence protects you sairlie;[2]   5
I canna say but ye strunt[3] rarely
    Owre gauze and lace;
Tho' faith! I fear ye dine but sparely
    On sic a place.

Ye ugly, creepin', blastet wonner,[4]   10
Detested, shunn'd by saunt an' sinner,
How daur ye set your fit[5] upon her,
    Sae fine a lady?
Gae somewhere else and seek your dinner
    On some poor body.   15

Swith![6] in some beggar's hauffet[7] squattle,[8]
Wi' ither kindred, jumping cattle,
There ye may creep, an' sprawl, an' sprattle,[9]
    In shoals and nations;
Whaur horn[10] or bane ne'er dare unsettle   20
    Your thick plantations.

Now haud you there, ye're out o' sight,
Below the fatt'rells,[11] snug an' tight;
Na, faith ye yet! ye'll no be right

---

[1] Where are you going, you crawling wonder?   [2] marvellously.   [3] strut.
[4] blasted wonder. [5] foot. [6] begone! [7] side of the head. [8] sprawl.
[9] scramble. [10] comb. [11] ribbon ends.

Till ye 've got on it —
The vera tapmost, towrin' height
O' Miss's bonnet.

My sooth ! right bauld [1] ye set your nose out,
As plump an' grey as ony groset : [2]
O for some rank, mercurial rozet, [3]
Or fell, red smeddum, [4]
I 'd gie ye sic a hearty dose o 't,
Wad dress your droddum ! [5]

I wad na been surpris'd to spy
You on an auld wife's flannen toy ; [6]
Or aiblins [7] some bit duddie [8] boy,
On 's wyliecoat ; [9]
But Miss's fine Lunardi ! [10] fye !
How daur ye do 't ?

O Jeany, dinna toss your head,
An' set your beauties a' abreid ! [11]
Ye little ken what cursed speed
The blastie 's [12] makin' :
Thae winks an' finger-ends, I dread,
Are notice takin. [13]

O wad some Power the giftie gie us
To see oursels as ithers see us !
It wad frae mony a blunder free us,
An' foolish notion :
What airs in dress an' gait wad lea'e us,
And ev'n devotion !

---

1 bold.   2 gooseberry.   3 rosin.   4 powder.   5 breech.   6 old-fashioned cap.
7 perhaps.   8 little ragged.   9 flannel vest.   10 balloon-shaped bonnet.
11 abroad.   12 as in the second stanza, a term of contempt; strictly,
"withered dwarf."   13 "I fear, from the way folk are winking and
pointing in your direction, that they see what is the matter."—*Wallace.*

Of course a man who habitually went out into the fields to compose his poetry could not ignore inanimate nature. If the subject of the following verses calls to mind Wordsworth's poems to the daisy and other flowers, we should remember that the Scottish plowman sang to his daisy first. 5

TO A MOUNTAIN DAISY,

ON TURNING ONE DOWN WITH THE PLOUGH, IN APRIL, 1786.

WEE, modest, crimson-tippèd flow'r,
Thou's met me in an evil hour;
For I maun crush amang the stoure[1]
      Thy slender stem: 10
To spare thee now is past my pow'r,
      Thou bonie gem.

Alas! it's no thy neibor sweet,
The bonie lark, companion meet,
Bending thee 'mang the dewy weet[2] 15
      Wi' spreckl'd breast,
When upward-springing, blythe, to greet
      The purpling east.

Cauld blew the bitter-biting north
Upon thy early, humble birth; 20
Yet cheerfully thou glinted forth
      Amid the storm,
Scarce rear'd above the parent-earth
      Thy tender form.

The flaunting flowers our gardens yield 25
High shelt'ring woods an' wa's[3] maun shield:

---

[1] dust.   [2] wet.   [3] walls.

But thou, beneath the random bield [1]
                    O' clod or stane,
Adorns the histie [2] stibble [3]-field
                    Unseen, alane.

5   There, in thy scanty mantle clad,
        Thy snawie [4] bosom sun-ward spread,
        Thou lifts thy unassuming head
                    In humble guise;
        But now the share uptears thy bed,
10   And low thou lies!

        Such is the fate of artless maid,
        Sweet flow'ret of the rural shade!
        By love's simplicity betray'd
                    And guileless trust;
15   Till she, like thee, all soil'd, is laid
                    Low i' the dust.

        Such is the fate of simple bard,
        On life's rough ocean luckless starr'd!
        Unskilful he to note the card [5]
20   Of prudent lore,
        Till billows rage and gales blow hard,
                    And whelm him o'er!

        Such fate to suffering Worth is giv'n,
        Who long with wants and woes has striv'n,
25   By human pride or cunning driv'n
                    To mis'ry's brink;
        Till, wrench'd of ev'ry stay but Heav'n,
                    He ruin'd sink!

---

1 shelter.   2 barren.   3 stubble.   4 snowy.   5 chart. "Reason the
card, but passion is the gale." — *Pope.*

Ev'n thou who mourn'st the Daisy's fate,
That fate is thine — no distant date;
Stern Ruin's ploughshare drives elate,
      Full on thy bloom,
Till crush'd beneath the furrow's weight   5
      Shall be thy doom.

  Burns was having a hard fight. The Mossgiel farming
had proved a failure. It looked as if Jean had deserted
him once for all and as if the marriage was annulled. With
wounded pride he looked for 'another wife' and soon 10
won the heart of Mary Campbell, of whom we know
through tradition only. (See "Highland Mary" and "To
Mary in Heaven.") This year, too, Burns had been
censured by the kirk. The result was his satires on the
Auld Licht clergy, which in turn met with local favor 15
enough to encourage him to continue his writing. It
seemed best to leave Scotland for the Indies, and he
published a collection of poems to pay the expenses of
the journey. The last poem in the volume speaks for
itself as a revelation of the poet's heart of hearts: 20

A BARD'S EPITAPH.

Is there a whim-inspirèd fool,
Owre fast for thought, owre hot for rule,
Owre blate[1] to seek, owre proud to snool?[2] —
    Let him draw near;
And owre this grassy heap sing dool,[3]   25
    And drap a tear.

Is there a bard of rustic song
Who, noteless, steals the crowds among,

---

[1] bashful.   [2] submit tamely.   [3] lament.

That weekly this aréa throng? —
　　　Oh, pass not by!
But with a frater-feeling strong,
　　　Here heave a sigh.

5　　Is there a man whose judgment clear
Can others teach the course to steer,
Yet runs himself life's mad career
　　　Wild as the wave? —
Here pause — and, thro' the starting tear
10　　　Survey this grave.

The poor inhabitant below
Was quick to learn and wise to know,
And keenly felt the friendly glow,
　　　And softer flame;
15　But thoughtless follies laid him low,
　　　And stain'd his name!

Reader, attend! whether thy soul
Soars fancy's flights beyond the pole,
Or darkling grubs this earthly hole
20　　　In low pursuit;
Know, prudent, cautious self-control
　　　Is wisdom's root.

After a man has written such an epitaph for himself —
so frankly disclosing and confessing his faults — it would
25 seem to be in good taste for the critics to save their
severest condemnation for one who is not so keenly
sensible of his shortcomings.

Soon afterward Burns met for the first time a member of
the British aristocracy. Lord Daer so pleasantly surprised
30 him that he at once acknowledged the unexpected in the

LINES ON AN INTERVIEW WITH LORD DAER.

THIS wot ye all whom it concerns,
I, Rhymer Robin, alias Burns,
      October twenty-third,
A ne'er-to-be-forgotten day,
Sae far I sprachled [1] up the brae,[2]   5
      I dinner'd wi' a Lord.

I 've been at drucken [3] writers' feasts,
Nay, been bitch-fou 'mang godly priests —
      Wi' rev'rence be it spoken! —
I 've even join'd the honour'd jorum,[4]
When mighty Squireships of the Quorum [5]   10
      Their hydra drouth [6] did sloken.[7]

But wi' a Lord — stand out my shin! [8]
A Lord — a Peer — an Earl's son!
      Up higher yet, my bonnet!
And sic a Lord — lang Scotch ells twa,[9]   15
Our Peerage he o'erlooks them a',
      As I look owre my sonnet.

But O for Hogarth's magic pow'r
To show Sir Bardie's willyart glow'r,[10]   20
      And how he star'd and stammer'd,
When goavan,[11] as if led wi' branks,[12]
An' stumpin on his ploughman shanks,
      He in the parlor hammer'd!

---

[1] scrambled.   [2] hill.   [3] drunken.   [4] punch-bowl.   [5] some board or committee representing the country gentlemen of Ayrshire. — *Wallace.*
[6] thirst.   [7] slake.   [8] as in a pompous stage-strut. — *Dow.*   [9] six feet tall.   [10] bewildered gaze.   [11] staring stupidly.   [12] bridle.

I sidling shelter'd in a nook,
An' at his Lordship steal't a look,
      Like some portentous omen;
Except good sense and social glee,
5   An' (what surprised me) modesty,
      I markèd nought uncommon.

I watch'd the symptoms o' the great,
The gentle pride, the lordly state,
      The arrogant assuming:
10   The fient a pride, nae pride had he,[1]
Nor sauce nor state that I could see,
      Mair than an honest ploughman.

Then from his lordship I shall learn,
Henceforth to meet with unconcern
15   One rank as weel 's another:
Nae honest worthy man need care
To meet with noble youthful Daer,
      For he but meets a brother.

    The first volume was welcomed so heartily that Burns
20 decided to remain on old Scotia's shores. . He had
attracted attention enough to make him more ambitious
than ever for distinction as a poet; he must go to Edinburgh. A few days before starting he sent these lines
to a gentleman in Ayr:

[1] 'Devil a bit of pride had he.'

A WINTER NIGHT.

Poor naked wretches, wheresoe'er you are,
That bide the pelting of this pitiless storm!
How shall your houseless heads and unfed sides,
Your loop'd and window'd raggedness, defend you
From seasons such as these?

SHAKESPEARE.

WHEN biting Boreas, fell [1] and doure, [2]
Sharp shivers thro' the leafless bow'r;
When Phœbus gies a short lived glow'r [3]
    Far south the lift, [4]
Dim-darkening thro' the flaky show'r   5
    Or whirling drift;

Ae night the storm the steeples rocked,
Poor Labour sweet in sleep was locked,
While burns, [5] wi' snawy wreaths up-choked,
    Wild-eddying swirl,
Or, thro' the mining outlet bocked, [6]   10
    Down headlong hurl:

Listening the doors and winnocks [7] rattle,
I thought me on the ourie [8] cattle,
Or silly [9] sheep, wha bide this brattle [10]   15
    O' winter war,
An' through the drift, deep-lairing, [11] sprattle [12]
    Beneath a scaur. [13]

Ilk happin [14] bird — wee, helpless thing! —
That in the merry months o' spring   20
Delighted me to hear thee sing,
    What comes o' thee?

[1] keen.   [2] stubborn.   [3] stare.   [4] sky.   [5] brooks.   [6] belched.   [7] windows.
[8] shivering.   [9] helpless.   [10] pelting.   [11] sinking deep.   [12] scramble.
[13] cliff.   [14] hopping.

Whare wilt thou cow'r thy chittering[1] wing
    An' close thy ee?

Ev'n you on murd'ring errands toil'd,
Lone from your savage homes exil'd, —
5 The blood-stain'd roost an' sheep-cot spoil'd
    My heart forgets,
While pitiless the tempest wild
    Sore on you beats.

Now Phœbe,[2] in her midnight reign,
10 Dark muffled, viewed the dreary plain;
Still crowding thoughts, a pensive train,
    Rose in my soul,
When on my ear this plaintive strain,
    Slow-solemn, stole: —

15 "Blow, blow ye winds with heavier gust!
And freeze, thou bitter-biting frost!
Descend, ye chilly, smothering snows!
Not all your rage, as now united, shows
    More hard unkindness, unrelenting,
20   Vengeful malice, unrepenting,
Than heaven-illumined man on brother man bestows![3]

"See stern Oppression's iron grip,
  Or mad Ambition's gory hand,
Sending, like blood-hounds from the slip,
25   Woe, Want, and Murder o'er a land!

---

[1] shivering.   [2] the moon.
[3] *Cf.* Blow, blow, thou winter wind,
    Thou art not so unkind
      As man's ingratitude; . . .
    Freeze, freeze, thou bitter sky,
    That dost not bite so nigh
      As benefits forgot. — *As You Like It*, II: 7.

Ev'n in the peaceful rural vale,
Truth, weeping, tells the mournful tale :
How pamper'd Luxury, Flatt'ry by her side,
The parasite empoisoning her ear,
With all the servile wretches in the rear,   5
Looks o'er proud Property, extended wide ;
And eyes the simple, rustic hind,
Whose toil upholds the glitt'ring show —
A creature of another kind,
Some coarser substance, unrefin'd —   10
Plac'd for her lordly use, thus far, thus vile, below !

"Where, where is Love's fond, tender throe,
With lordly Honour's lofty brow,
The pow'rs you proudly own ?
Is there, beneath Love's noble name,   15
Can harbour, dark, the selfish aim,
To bless himself alone ?
Mark Maiden-Innocence a prey
To love-pretending snares :
This boasted Honour turns away,   20
Shunning soft Pity's rising sway,
Regardless of the tears and unavailing pray'rs !
Perhaps this hour, in Misery's squalid nest,
She strains your infant to her joyless breast,
And with a mother's fears shrinks at the rocking blast ! 25

"O ye ! who, sunk in beds of down,
Feel not a want but what yourselves create,
Think, for a moment, on his wretched fate,
Whom friends and fortune quite disown !
Ill-satisfy'd keen nature's clam'rous call,   30
Stretched on his straw, he lays himself to sleep ;
While through the ragged roof and chinky wall,

Chill, o'er his slumbers piles the drifty heap!
Think on the dungeon's grim confine,
Where Guilt and poor Misfortune pine!
Guilt, erring man, relenting view!
5   But shall thy legal rage pursue
The wretch, already crushèd low
By cruel Fortune's undeservèd blow?
Affliction's sons are brothers in distress;
A brother to relieve, how exquisite the bliss!"

10   I heard nae mair, for chanticleer
Shook off the pouthery [1] snaw,
And hailed the morning with a cheer—
A cottage-rousing craw.

But deep this truth impress'd my mind—
15   Through all His works abroad,
The heart benevolent and kind
The most resembles God.[2]

The difference between the Scottish and the English
portions of the poem is striking. This is "the voice of
20 Mercy herself," says Carlyle.

It was on the 28th of November, 1786, that Burns
reached Edinburgh and began his triumphal winter. The
following summer he traveled in Scotland; the Highlands
set him to singing. One of these songs is

THE BANKS OF THE DEVON.

25 How pleasant the banks of the clear winding Devon,
With green spreading bushes, and flowers blooming fair!

---

[1] powdery.   [2] *Cf.* "He prayeth best who loveth best" etc.
— *Ancient Mariner.*

But the boniest flower on the banks of the Devon
    Was once a sweet bud on the braes [1] of the Ayr.[2]
Mild be the sun on this sweet blushing flower,
    In the gay rosy morn as it bathes in the dew;
And gentle the fall of the soft vernal shower,
    That steals on the evening each leaf to renew.   5

O spare the dear blossom, ye orient breezes,
    With chill hoary wing as ye usher the dawn!
And far be thou distant, thou reptile that seizes
    The verdure and pride of the garden and lawn!   10.
Let Bourbon exult in his gay gilded lilies,
    And England, triumphant, display her proud rose;
A fairer than either adorns the green valleys,
    Where Devon, sweet Devon, meandering flows.

In a letter to Miss Chalmers, Burns says: "The air 15
is admirable : true old Highland.   It was the tune of a
Gaelic song which an Inverness lady sang me when I
was there. . . .   I won't say the poetry is first-rate;
though I am convinced it is very well: and what is not
always the case with compliments to ladies, it is not only 20
sincere but *just*."

Another song which was a direct outcome of the Highland tour is

M'PHERSON'S FAREWELL.

Farewell, ye dungeons dark and strong,
    The wretch's destinie!
M'Pherson's time will not be long   25
    On yonder gallows tree.

---

[1] slopes.   [2] "Miss Charlotte Hamilton . . . was born on the banks of the Ayr,
but was, at the time I wrote these lines, residing at Harvieston, on the
romantic banks of the little river Devon." — *B.*

CHORUS. — Sae rantinly, sae wantonly,
      Sae dauntinly gaed he;
      He play'd a spring[1] and danc'd it round,
        Below the gallows tree.

5   O what is death but parting breath? —
       On monie a bloody plain
    I 've dar'd his face, and in this place
       I scorn him yet again!

    Untie these bands from off my hands
10   And bring to me my sword,
    And there 's no man in all Scotland,
       But I 'll brave him at a word.

    I 've liv'd a life of sturt[2] and strife;
       I die by treacherie:
15   It burns my heart I must depart
       And not avengèd be.

    Now farewell light, thou sunshine bright,
       And all beneath the sky!
    May coward shame distain[3] his name,
20   The wretch that dare not die!

James M'Pherson, a freebooter, who with his Gypsy followers terrified the Counties of Aberdeen, Moray, and Banff, was finally seized and condemned to be hanged. While in prison, it is said, he composed the wild air which 25 prompted Burns to write this song.

The next winter, which was spent in Edinburgh, the worshipers were fewer and some of them far less enthusiastic. In the spring Burns leased a poor farm at

---

1 piece of dance music.   2 trouble.   3 stain.

Ellisland, and was regularly married to Jean Armour. While she was visiting his mother and sisters at Mossgiel and learning how to do her part of the work on the new farm, he was preparing the home. Meantime this is his song to her : 5

OF A' THE AIRTS THE WIND CAN BLAW.

Of a' the airts [1] the wind can blaw
　I dearly like the west,
For there the bonie lassie lives,
　The lassie I lo'e best :
There 's wild woods grow an' rivers row, [2]　10
　An' mony a hill between ;
But day and night my fancy's flight
　Is ever wi' my Jean.

I see her in the dewy flow'rs,
　I see her sweet an' fair :　15
I hear her in the tunefu' birds,
　I hear her charm the air :
There 's not a bonie flow'r that springs
　By fountain, shaw, [3] or green ;
There 's not a bonie bird that sings,　20
　But minds me o' my Jean.

And who, with or without an ear for music, does not like such singing ?

Again winter had come, and it had brought Jean. As farmer and exciseman Burns struggled on. He sent Mrs. 25 Dunlop

---

[1] directions.　[2] roll.　[3] wood.

AULD LANG SYNE.

SHOULD auld acquaintance be forgot,
        And never brought to min'?
Should auld acquaintance be forgot,
        And auld lang syne?

5 CHORUS.—For auld lang syne, my dear,
        For auld lang syne,
    We 'll tak a cup o' kindness yet
        For auld lang syne.

And surely ye 'll be your pint-stowp,[1]
10   And surely I 'll be mine!
And we 'll tak a cup o' kindness yet
        For auld lang syne.

We twa hae run about the braes,
        And pu'd the gowans fine;[2]
15 But we 've wander'd mony a weary fit[3]
        Sin' auld lang syne.

We twa hae paidl't[4] i' the burn,[5]
        From mornin' sun till dine;[6]
But seas between us braid[7] hae roar'd
20   Sin' auld lang syne.

And there 's a hand, my trusty fier,[8]
        And gie 's a hand o' thine;
And we 'll tak a right guid-willie waught[9]
        For auld lang syne.

25 It is the favorite song at reunions among the Scots.
Although there are several versions of it, Burns's work
is conspicuous in his third and fourth stanzas.

1 drinking vessel.   2 pulled daisies.   3 foot.   4 paddled.   5 brook.
6 dinner-time.   7 broad.   8 comrade.   9 friendly draught.

In this connection it ought to be said that we are indebted to him for improving many an old song. One to which his re-working gave purity, life, and beauty is

JOHN ANDERSON MY JO.

JOHN ANDERSON my jo,[1] John,
　When we were first acquent,
Your locks were like the raven,
　Your bonie[2] brow was brent;
But now your brow is beld,[3] John,
　Your locks are like the snaw;
But blessings on your frosty pow,[4]
　John Anderson my jo.

John Anderson my jo, John,
　We clamb the hill thegither;
And monie a canty[5] day, John,
　We 've had wi' ane anither:
Now we maun totter down, John,
　And hand in hand we 'll go,
And sleep thegither at the foot,
　John Anderson my jo.

The story of two long lives is told so briefly that a hasty glance is not likely to reveal the perfection of the little gem. As with the man John Anderson, acquaintance increases the liking.

In the illustration which accompanied the song in Thomson's work "the old couple are seated by the fireside, the gude-wife in great good humor is clapping John's shoulder, while he smiles and looks at her with such glee as to show that he fully recollects the pleasant days when

---

[1] sweetheart.　[2] high and straight.　[3] bald.　[4] head.　[5] happy.

they were 'first acquent.'" [Letter of Thomson to Burns, 1793.] On the other hand, Mr. Wallace says: "The pathos of life's evening will never find a happier or fuller expression." To me the poem does not suggest 5 "great good humor," nor is the keynote pathos. Some of the lines may not be free from pathos, but the touch only heightens the happiness. It is thoughtful, serene, supreme happiness.

The air of the next song was Masterton's, Burns 10 says; the song, his. "The occasion of it," he adds, "was this: Mr. William Nicol, of the High School, Edinburgh, during the autumn vacation being at Moffat, honest Allan [Masterton] and I went to pay Nicol a visit. We had such a joyous meeting that Mr. Masterton and I agreed, 15 each in our own way, that we should celebrate the business."

WILLIE BREWED A PECK O' MAUT.

O, WILLIE brew'd a peck o' maut,[1]
　　An' Rob an' Allan cam to see:
　　Three blyther hearts that lee-lang night
20　　　Ye wad na found in Christendie.

CHORUS.—We are na fou, we're nae that fou,[2]
　　　　But just a drappie[3] in our ee;[4]
　　　　The cock may craw, the day may daw,[5]
　　　　And aye we'll taste the barley bree.[6]

25　　　Here are we met, three merry boys,
　　　Three merry boys, I trow, are we;
　　　An' mony a night we've merry been,
　　　An mony mae[7] we hope to be!

　·　[1] malt.　[2] full.　[3] drop.　[4] eye.　[5] dawn.　[6] liquor.　[7] more.

It is the moon, I ken her horn,
  That 's blinkin [1] in the lift [2] sae hie; [3]
She shines sae bright to wile us hame,
  But, by my sooth, she 'll wait a wee!

Wha first shall rise to gang awa',   5
  A cuckold, coward loon [4] is he!
Wha first beside his chair shall fa',
  He is the king amang us three!

The following stanzas were written to Mary Campbell, whose lover he had become three years before. [5] The [10] third anniversary of her death saddened him. He spent most of the cold night wandering on the banks of the Nith and about his farmyard. Lockhart, in reporting a statement made by Jean Burns to a friend, says his wife finally found him "stretched on a mass of straw with his eyes [15] fixed on a beautiful planet 'that shone like another moon' and prevailed on him to come in. He immediately . . . wrote . . . with all the ease of one copying from memory, these sublime and pathetic verses":

TO MARY IN HEAVEN.

THOU ling'ring star, with less'ning ray,   20
  That lov'st to greet the early morn,
Again thou usher'st in the day
  My Mary from my soul was torn.
O Mary! dear departed shade!
  Where is thy place of blissful rest?   25
See'st thou thy lover lowly laid?
  Hear'st thou the groans that rend his breast?

[1] gleaming.   [2] sky.   [3] high.   [4] fellow.   [5] See introduction to
A Bard's Epitaph.

That sacred hour can I forget,
    Can I forget the hallowed grove,
Where by the winding Ayr we met
    To live one day of parting love?
5   Eternity will not efface
    Those records dear of transports past,
Thy image at our last embrace—
    Ah! little thought we 't was our last!

Ayr, gurgling, kiss'd his pebbl'd shore,
10   O'erhung with wild woods, thick'ning green;
The fragrant birch and hawthorn hoar
    Twin'd amorous round the raptur'd scene:
The flow'rs sprang wanton to be prest,
    The birds sang love on every spray,
15   Till too, too soon the glowing west
    Proclaim'd the speed of winged day.

Still o'er these scenes my mem'ry wakes,
    And fondly broods with miser care!
Time but th' impression stronger makes,
20   As streams their channels deeper wear.
My Mary, dear departed shade!
    Where is thy place of blissful rest?
See'st thou thy lover lowly laid?
    Hear'st thou the groans that rend his breast?

25   While Captain Grose, the antiquary, was preparing his
Antiquities of Scotland, Burns asked him to include Alloway Kirk, the burial-place of the poet's father, and the
scene of many good witch stories. The captain agreed
to make the drawing, provided Burns would furnish an
30 accompanying legend. The result was that Burns wrote
three prose stories and turned one of them into

TAM O' SHANTER.

A TALE.

Of Brownyis and of Bogillis full is this Buke. — GAWIN DOUGLAS.

WHEN chapman billies leave the street,[1]
And drouthy[2] neibors neibors meet,
As market-days are wearing late,
And folk begin to tak the gate;[3]
While we sit bousin[4] at the nappy,[5]   5
And gettin fou[6] and unco happy,
We think na on the lang Scots miles,
The mosses, waters, slaps,[7] and stiles,
That lie between us and our hame,
Whare sits our sulky, sullen dame,   10
Gathering her brows like gathering storm,
Nursing her wrath to keep it warm.

This truth fand[8] honest Tam o' Shanter,
As he frae Ayr ae night did canter:
(Auld Ayr, wham ne'er a town surpasses,   15
For honest men and bonie lasses.)

O Tam! had'st thou but been sae wise
As taen thy ain wife Kate's advice!
She tauld thee weel thou was a skellum,
A bletherin, blusterin, drunken blellum;   20
That frae November till October,
Ae market-day[9] thou was na sober;
That ilka[10] melder[11] wi' the miller,
Thou sat as lang as thou had siller;

---

[1] When packman fellows, the sellers at the booths and stalls, leave the market. [2] thirsty. [3] road. [4] drinking deeply. [5] ale. [6] full. [7] bogs. [8] found. [9] the weekly market. [10] every. [11] the quantity of grain sent to the mill to be ground at one time.

That ev'ry naig[1] was ca'd a shoe on,[2]
The smith and thee gat roarin fou on;
That at the Lord's house, ev'n on Sunday,
Thou drank wi' Kirkton[3] Jean till Monday.

5   She prophesied, that, late or soon,
Thou would be found deep drown'd in Doon;
Or catch't wi' warlocks[4] in the mirk,[5]
By Alloway's auld haunted kirk.

    Ah, gentle dames! it gars[6] me greet,[7]
10 To think how mony counsels sweet,
How mony lengthened sage advices,
The husband frae the wife despises!

    But to our tale:— Ae market night,
Tam had got planted unco right,
15 Fast by an ingle[8] bleezin[9] finely,
Wi' reamin swats[10] that drank divinely;
And at his elbow, Souter[11] Johnie,
His ancient, trusty, drouthy[12] crony:
Tam lo'ed him like a vera brither;
20 They had been fou for weeks thegither.
The night drave on wi' sangs and clatter;
And ay the ale was growing better:
The landlady and Tam grew gracious
Wi' secret favours, sweet, and precious:
25 The souter tauld his queerest stories;
The landlord's laugh was ready chorus:
The storm without might rair[13] and rustle,
Tam did na mind the storm a whistle.

---

[1] nag.   [2] shod.   [3] a common name for any country town that has a parish church. Here, perhaps, it means Kirkoswald, which claims the originals of all the characters in the poem.   [4] wizards.   [5] darkness. [6] makes.   [7] weep.   [8] fire.   [9] blazing.   [10] foaming ale.   [11] cobbler. [12] thirsty.   [13] roar.

Care, mad to see a man sae happy,
E'en drown'd himsel amang the nappy:
As bees flee hame wi' lades o' treasure,
The minutes wing'd their way wi' pleasure;
Kings may be blest, but Tam was glorious,   5
O'er a' the ills o' life victorious !

But pleasures are like poppies spread,
You seize the flow'r, its bloom is shed;
Or like the snow falls in the river,
A moment white — then melts for ever;   10
Or like the borealis race,
That flit e'er you can point their place;
Or like the rainbow's lovely form
Evanishing amid the storm.
Nae man can tether time or tide: 15
The hour approaches Tam maun ride, —
That hour, o' night's black arch the key-stane,
That dreary hour he mounts his beast in;
And sic a night he taks the road in,
As ne'er poor sinner was abroad in.   20

The wind blew as 't wad blawn its last;
The rattling show'rs rose on the blast;
The speedy gleams the darkness swallow'd;
Loud, deep, and lang the thunder bellow'd:
That night, a child might understand,   25
The Deil had business on his hand.[1]

Weel mounted on his gray mear,[2] Meg,
A better never lifted leg,

[1] Carlyle says that the "chasm between the Ayr public-house and the gate
of Tophet" — between the natural and the supernatural — "is nowhere
bridged over." It has been suggested that line 8, page 64, is the first
link and that these two are the second.   [2] mare.

Tam skelpit[1] on thro' dub[2] and mire,
Despising wind and rain and fire;
Whiles holding fast his guid blue bonnet,
Whiles crooning o'er some auld Scots sonnet,
5   Whiles glowrin round wi' prudent cares,
Lest bogles catch him unawares.
Kirk-Alloway was drawing nigh,
Whare ghaists and houlets[3] nightly cry.

By this time he was cross the ford,
10   Whare in the snaw the chapman smoor'd;[4]
And past the birks[5] and meikle[6] stane,
Whare drucken Charlie brak 's neck-bane;
And thro' the whins,[7] and by the cairn,[8]
Whare hunters fand the murder'd bairn;
15   And near the thorn, aboon the well,
Whare Mungo's mither hang'd hersel.
Before him Doon pours all his floods;
The doubling storm roars thro' the woods;
The lightnings flash from pole to pole,
20   Near and more near the thunders roll;
When, glimmering thro' the groaning trees,
Kirk-Alloway[9] seemed in a bleeze;
Thro' ilka bore[10] the beams were glancing,
And loud resounded mirth and dancing.

25   Inspiring bold John Barleycorn!
What dangers thou can'st make us scorn!
Wi' tippenny[11] we fear nae evil;
Wi' usquebae[12] we 'll face the devil!

---

[1] rattled.   [2] puddle.   [3] owls.   [4] smothered.   [5] birches.   [6] big.   [7] gorse.
[8] pile of stones.   [9] Burns was born within a few yards of this church. Though deserted in his time, it was prominent in many of the stories of devils, ghosts, and witches told Burns by the superstitious old woman who lived in the family. Now it is a roofless ruin.   [10] crevice.
[11] twopenny ale.   [12] whiskey.

The swats sae ream'd in Tammie's noddle,
Fair play, he car'd na deils a boddle.
But Maggie stood right sair astonish'd,
Till, by the heel and hand admonish'd,
She ventur'd forward on the light ;   5
And, wow ! Tam saw an unco sight !

Warlocks[1] and witches in a dance ;
Nae cotillon brent new[2] frae France,
But hornpipes, jigs, strathspeys, and reels
Put life and mettle in their heels :   10
A winnock[3] bunker[4] in the east,
There sat Auld Nick in shape o' beast ;
A towzie tyke,[5] black, grim, and large,
To gie them music was his charge ;
He screw'd the pipes[6] and gart them skirl,[7]   15
Till roof and rafters a' did dirl.[8] —
Coffins stood round like open presses,
That shaw'd the dead in their last dresses ;
And by some devilish cantraip sleight[9]
Each in its cauld hand held a light,   20
By which heroic Tam was able
To note upon the haly table[10]
A murderer's banes in gibbet airns ;[11]
Twa span-lang, wee, unchristen'd bairns ;
A thief, new-cutted frae the rape —   25
Wi' his last gasp his gab[12] did gape ;
Five tomahawks, wi' blude red-rusted ;
Five scymitars, wi' murder crusted ;
A garter, which a babe had strangled ;
A knife, a father's throat had mangled,   30

[1] wizards.   [2] brand-new.   [3] window.   [4] recess.   [5] shaggy dog.   [6] bagpipes.
[7] scream.   [8] ring.   [9] weird trick.   [10] communion table.   [11] irons.
[12] mouth.

Whom his ain son o' life bereft —
The gray hairs yet stack [1] to the heft; [2]
Wi' mair o' horrible and awfu', [3]
Which ev'n to name wad be unlawfu'.

5   As Tammie glowr'd, amaz'd and curious,
The mirth and fun grew fast and furious :
The piper loud and louder blew,
The dancers quick and quicker flew ;
They reel'd, they set, they cross'd, they cleekit, [4]
10   Till ilka carlin [5] swat and reekit [6]
And coost [7] her duddies [8] to the wark
And linket at it [9] in her sark ! [10]

     Now Tam, O Tam ! had thae [11] been queans, [12]
A' plump and strapping in their teens !
15   Their sarks, instead o' creeshie flannen, [13]
Been snaw-white seventeen hunder linen ! [14] —
Thir [15] breeks o' mine, my only pair,
That ance were plush, o' gude blue hair,
I wad hae gien them aff my hurdies, [16]
20   For ae blink o' the bonie burdies ! [17]

     But wither'd beldams, auld and droll,
Rigwoodie [18] hags wad spean [19] a foal,
Lowping [20] and flinging on a crummock, [21]
I wonder didna turn thy stomach.

25   But Tam ken'd what was what fu' brawlie; [22]
There was ae winsome wench and walie, [23]

---

[1] stuck.   [2] handle.   [3] Cf. *Macbeth*, IV, I.   [4] joined hands.   [5] witch.
[6] steamed.   [7] threw off.   [8] clothes.   [9] set to it.   [10] shift.   [11] those.
[12] young women.   [13] greasy flannel.   [14] very fine linen, woven in a
reed of seventeen hundred divisions.   [15] these.   [16] hips.   [17] damsels.
[18] wizened.   [19] wean.   [20] leaping.   [21] staff with a crooked head.
[22] very well.   [23] powerful.

That night enlisted in the core [1]
(Lang after ken'd on Carrick shore:
For mony a beast to dead she shot,
And perish'd mony a bonie boat,
And shook baith meikle corn and bear,[2] 5
And kept the country-side in fear);
Her cutty sark o' Paisley harn, [3]
That while a lassie she had worn,
In longitude tho' sorely scanty,
It was her best, and she was vauntie.[4] 10
Ah! little kent thy reverend grannie,
That sark she coft [5] for her wee Nannie,
Wi' twa pund Scots ('t was a' her riches),
Wad ever graced a dance o' witches!

But here my Muse her wing maun cow'r,[6] 15
Sic flights are far beyond her pow'r;
To sing how Nannie lap and flang,[7]
(A souple jad [8] she was and strang,)
And how Tam stood like ane bewitch'd,
And thought his very een enrich'd; 20
Even Satan glowr'd [9] and fidg'd fu' fain,
And hotch'd [10] and blew wi' might and main:
Till first ae caper, syne [11] anither,
Tam tint [12] his reason a' thegither,
And roars out, "Weel done, Cutty-sark!" 25
And in an instant all was dark:
And scarcely had he Maggie rallied,
When out the hellish legion sallied.

As bees bizz out wi' angry fyke,[13]
When plundering herds assail their byke;[14] 30

---

[1] company. [2] barley. [3] short shift of coarse linen. [4] proud of it. [5] bought.
[6] fold. [7] leaped and kicked. [8] lass. [9] gazed. [10] moved uneasily.
[11] then. [12] lost. [13] fuss. [14] nest.

As open pussie's [1] mortal foes,
When, pop! she starts before their nose;
As eager runs the market-crowd,
When "Catch the thief!" resounds aloud;
So Maggie runs, the witches follow,
Wi' mony an eldritch [2] skriech and hollo.

Ah, Tam! ah, Tam! thou'll get thy fairin! [3]
In hell they'll roast thee like a herrin!
In vain thy Kate awaits thy comin!
Kate soon will be a woefu' woman!
Now, do thy speedy utmost, Meg,
And win the key-stane [4] of the brig:
There at them thou thy tail may toss,
A running stream they dare na cross.
But ere the key-stane she could make,
The fient a tail she had to shake!
For Nannie, far before the rest,
Hard upon noble Maggie prest,
And flew at Tam wi' furious ettle; [5]
But little wist she Maggie's mettle —
Ae spring brought aff her master hale,
But left behind her ain gray tail:
The carlin [6] claught [7] her by the rump,
And left poor Maggie scarce a stump.

Now, wha this tale o' truth shall read,
Ilk man and mother's son, take heed,

---

[1] the hare's.   [2] unearthly.   [3] reward.   [4] It is a well known fact that witches, or any evil spirits, have no power to follow a poor wight any farther than the middle of the next running stream. It may be proper likewise to mention to the benighted traveller, that when he falls in with *bogles*, whatever danger may be in his going forward, there is much more hazard in turning back. — *B.*   [5] aim.   [6] witch.   [7] clutched.

Whene'er to drink you are inclin'd,
    Or cutty-sarks run in your mind,
Think, ye may buy the joys owre dear,
    Remember Tam o' Shanter's mear.[1]

" *Tam o' Shanter*," says Burns, "is my first essay in 5
the way of telling a tale." It is his only tale and in the
opinion of Scott, Lockhart, Burns himself, and perhaps
a majority of Scots, his masterpiece. It is said to have
been written in one day. Carlyle says it is "the best
day's work done in Scotland since Bannockburn."   10
    A lyric that needs no comment is

BONIE DOON.

YE flowery banks o' bonie Doon,
    How can ye blume sae fair?
How can ye chant, ye little birds,
    And I sae fu' o' care?   15

Thou 'll break my heart, thou bonie bird,
    That sings upon the bough;
Thou minds me o' the happy days,
    When my fause luve was true.

Thou 'll break my heart, thou bonie bird,   20
    That sings beside thy mate;
For sae I sat, and sae I sang,
    And wist na o' my fate.

[1] It is interesting to compare the ending of the prose version : "However, the
unsightly, tail-less condition of the vigorous steed was to the last hour
of the noble creature's life an awful warning to all Carrick farmers not
to stay too late in Ayr markets."

Aft hae I rov'd by bonie Doon
    To see the wood-bine twine,
And ilka[1] bird sang o' its luve,
    And sae did I o' mine.

5   Wi' lightsome heart I pu'd a rose
    Frae aff its thorny tree;
And my fause luver staw[2] my rose
    But left the thorn wi' me.

The result is so good that one may be surprised to learn
10 from Mr. Scott Douglas that the poet's aim in composing
"this most popular of his songs" was merely to fit a particular tune with suitable words.

Again, we do not know the heroine of

FLOW GENTLY, SWEET AFTON.

FLOW gently, sweet Afton, among thy green braes,[3]
15 Flow gently, I 'll sing thee a song in thy praise;
My Mary's asleep by thy murmuring stream,
Flow gently, sweet Afton, disturb not her dream.

Thou stock-dove whose echo resounds thro' the glen,
Ye wild whistling blackbirds in yon thorny den,
20 Thou green-crested lapwing, thy screaming forbear,
I charge you disturb not my slumbering fair.

How lofty, sweet Afton, thy neighbouring hills,
Far mark'd with the courses of clear winding rills;
There daily I wander as noon rises high,
25 My flocks and my Mary's sweet cot in my eye.

[1] every.   [2] stole.   [3] slopes.

How pleasant thy banks and green valleys below,
Where wild in the woodlands the primroses blow;
There oft, as mild Evening weeps over the lea,
The sweet-scented birk [1] shades my Mary and me.

Thy crystal stream, Afton, how lovely it glides, 5
And winds by the cot where my Mary resides;
How wanton thy waters her snowy feet lave,
As gathering sweet flow'rets she stems thy clear wave.

Flow gently, sweet Afton, among thy green braes,
Flow gently, sweet river, the theme of my lays; 10
My Mary's asleep by thy murmuring stream,
Flow gently, sweet Afton, disturb not her dream.

It is not difficult to understand Mr. Douglas's note:
"A kind of holy calm pervades the soul of the reader
who peruses, or the auditor who listens to the music of 15
this unique strain. The 'pastoral melancholy' which
Wordsworth felt at St. Mary's Loch steals over his heart
and laps him in a dreamy elysium of sympathetic repose."

In 1787–8, before Burns's regular marriage with Jean
Armour, he had become acquainted with Mrs. Maclehose. 20
They found each other most fascinating. Their lively
correspondence came to an abrupt end, however, when
Burns told her of his coming marriage. In 1791 they
met again in time for Burns to bid her farewell before she
sailed to the West Indies. Soon afterward he sent her 25
the poem

---

[1] birch.

AE FOND KISS.

Ae fond kiss, and then we sever;
Ae fareweel, and then for ever!
Deep in heart-wrung tears I 'll pledge thee,
Warring sighs and groans I 'll wage thee.
5   Who shall say that Fortune grieves him,
While the star of hope she leaves him?
Me, nae cheerfu' twinkle lights me;
Dark despair around benights me.

I 'll ne'er blame my partial fancy,
10   Naething could resist my Nancy;
But to see her was to love her;
Love but her, and love for ever.
Had we never lov'd sae kindly,
Had we never lov'd sae blindly,
15   Never met — or never parted —
We had ne'er been broken-hearted.

Fare thee weel, thou first and fairest!
Fare thee weel, thou best and dearest!
Thine be ilka joy and treasure,
20   Peace, enjoyment, love, and pleasure!
Ae fond kiss, and then we sever;
Ae fareweel, alas, for ever!
Deep in heart-wrung tears I 'll pledge thee,
Warring sighs and groans I 'll wage [1] thee!

25   Scott has remarked that the four lines beginning with
"Had we never lov'd sae kindly" are worth a thousand
romances; and Mrs. Jameson has said that not only are
they worth a thousand romances — they are "in them-

[1] pledge.

selves a complete romance. They are the alpha and omega of feeling, and contain the essence of an existence of pain and pleasure distilled into one burning drop."

In August, 1792, Mr. Baillie and his two daughters, neighbors of Mrs. Dunlop, while on their way to England 5 called on Burns. The meeting with Miss Leslie Baillie filled the poet's soul with "delighting" and "pure" emotions, as he wrote Mrs. Dunlop. He accompanied his guests some fifteen miles, and as he rode home he thought of the old ballad beginning 10

> "O bonie Lizzie Baillie,
>   I 'll rowe thee in my plaidie,"

and composed

BONIE LESLEY.

O SAW ye bonie Lesley
    As she gaed o'er the border? 15
She 's gane, like Alexander,
    To spread her conquests farther.

To see her is to love her,
    And love but her for ever;
For Nature made her what she is, 20
    And never made anither !

Thou art a queen, fair Lesley,
    Thy subjects, we before thee:
Thou art divine, fair Lesley,
    The hearts o' men adore thee. 25

The Deil he could na scaith [1] thee,
    Or aught that wad belang thee;

[1] harm.

He 'd look into thy bonie face,
    And say, " I canna wrang thee."

The powers aboon will tent thee ;
    Misfortune sha' na steer [1] thee ;
5   Thou 'rt like themselves sae lovely,
    That ill they 'll ne'er let near thee.

Return again, fair Lesley,
    Return to Caledonie !
That we may brag, we hae a lass
10   There 's nane again sae bonie.

Three years before he had written *To Mary in Heaven.*
It is the same Mary that he remembers so tenderly in

HIGHLAND MARY.

YE banks, and braes, and streams around
    The castle o' Montgomery,
15 Green be your woods and fair your flowers,
    Your waters never drumlie ! [2]
There simmer [3] first unfauld her robes,
    And there the langest tarry ;
For there I took the last fareweel
20   O' my sweet Highland Mary.

How sweetly bloom'd the gay green birk,
    How rich the hawthorn's blossom,
As underneath their fragrant shade
    I clasp'd her to my bosom !
25 The golden hours, on angel wings,
    Flew o'er me and my dearie ;

---

[1] molest.   [2] muddy.   [3] summer.

For dear to me as light and life,
　Was my sweet Highland Mary.

Wi' monie a vow and lock'd embrace
　Our parting was fu' tender;
And, pledging aft to meet again,　　　　5
　We tore oursels asunder;
But O! fell death's untimely frost,
　That nipt my flower sae early!
Now green 's the sod, and cauld 's the clay,
　That wraps my Highland Mary!　　　　10

O pale, pale now, those rosy lips,
　I aft hae kiss'd sae fondly!
And closed for aye the sparkling glance,
　That dwelt on me sae kindly!
And mould'ring now in silent dust,　　　15
　That heart that lo'ed me dearly!
But still within my bosom's core
　Shall live my Highland Mary.

In the fall of this year, 1792, he began to send contributions to *Melodies of Scotland.*   He writes the editor, 20
Thomson: "I have hitherto deferred the sublimer, more
pathetic airs, until more leisure, as they will take and
deserve a greater effort."   And a week later he writes of
Highland Mary: "I think it in my happiest manner: you
will see at first glance that it suits the air," — Katherine 25
Ogie, one of the oldest and most plaintive of Scottish
melodies.

These verses illustrate Milton's declaration that rhyme
is "no necessary adjunct or true ornament of poem or
good verse."　　　　　　　　　　　　　　　　30

Another contribution to Thomson's collection was

DUNCAN GRAY.

DUNCAN GRAY came here to woo,
        Ha, ha, the wooin o 't!
On blythe Yule night when we were fou,
        Ha, ha, the wooin o 't !
5 Maggie coost her head fu hiegh,
Look'd asklent[1] and unco skiegh,[2]
Gart[3] poor Duncan stand abiegh;[4]
        Ha, ha, the wooin o 't!

Duncan fleech'd,[5] and Duncan pray'd;
10   Ha, ha, the wooin o 't!
Meg was deaf as Ailsa Craig,[6]
        Ha, ha, the wooin o 't !
Duncan sigh'd baith out and in,
Grat[7] his een[8] baith bleer't[9] and blin',
15 Spak o' lowpin owre a linn;[10]
        Ha, ha, the wooin o 't !

Time and chance are but a tide,
        Ha, ha, the wooin o 't!
Slighted love is sair to bide,
20   Ha, ha, the wooin o 't!
"Shall I, like a fool," quoth he,
"For a haughty hizzie[11] die?
She may gae to — France for me!"
        Ha, ha, the wooin o 't !

---

[1] askance.   [2] very high-spirited.   [3] made.   [4] aloof.   [5] flattered.   [6] a rocky
islet in the Firth of Clyde, near the Ayrshire coast.   [7] wept.   [8] eyes.
[9] bleared.   [10] *I.e.*, using drowning as a means of suicide. A linn is a
waterfall. "A line . . . that should make you immortal," wrote Hon.
Andrew Erskine to the poet.   [11] lass.

How it comes let doctors tell,
  Ha, ha, the wooin o 't !
Meg grew sick as he grew hale,
  Ha, ha, the wooin o 't !
Something in her bosom wrings,   5
For relief a sigh she brings ;
And O ! her een, they spak sic things !
  Ha, ha, the wooin o 't !

Duncan was a lad o' grace,
  Ha, ha, the wooin o 't !   10
Maggie's was a piteous case,
  Ha, ha, the wooin o 't !
Duncan could na be her death,
Swelling pity smoor'd[1] his wrath ;
Now they 're crouse and cantie[2] baith ; 15
  Ha, ha, the wooin o 't !

In sending this song to the editor, Burns writes : "'Duncan Gray' is that kind of light-horse gallop of an air which precludes sentiment. The ludicrous is its ruling feature." Mr. Douglas says : "Few of Burns's songs acquired a more rapid popularity than this ; it is so thoroughly pointed and natural throughout."

In 1791 Burns had given up his farm and bought a house in Dumfries, where he lived as exciseman. At this time his democratic sympathies were touched by the French Revolution. In 1793 some recent success of the "patriots," together with the recollection of Scotland's struggle for freedom in 1314, when Bruce on the field of Bannockburn gained the victory over Edward II which decided the independence of Scotland, roused Burns to write

---

[1] smothered. [2] lively and happy.

SCOTS WHA HAE.

Scots, wha hae wi' Wallace bled,
Scots, wham Bruce has aften led;
Welcome to your gory bed,
   Or to victory!
5   Now's the day, and now's the hour;
See the front o' battle lour;
See approach proud Edward's power —
   Chains and slavery!

Wha will be a traitor knave?
10   Wha can fill a coward's grave?
Wha sae base as be a slave?
   Let him turn and flee!
Wha for Scotland's king and law
Freedom's sword will strongly draw,
15   Freeman stand, or Freeman fa',
   Let him follow me!

By oppression's woes and pains!
By your sons in servile chains!
We will drain our dearest veins,
20   But they shall be free!
Lay the proud usurpers low!
Tyrants fall in every foe!
Liberty's in every blow! —
   Let us do, or die!

25   In sending Thomson this "Scot's Ode," which one
might suppose to be Bruce's "address to his heroic followers on that eventful morning," Burns added: "So
may God ever defend the cause of Truth and Liberty, as
He did that day!"

" Independently of my enthusiasm as a Scotsman," he wrote Lord Buchan, in 1794, "I have rarely met with anything in history which interests my feelings as a man, equal with the story of Bannockburn. On the one hand, a cruel, but able usurper, leading on the finest army in Europe, to extinguish the last spark of freedom among a greatly-daring and greatly-injured people; on the other hand, the desperate relics of a gallant nation devoting themselves to rescue their bleeding country or perish with her. Liberty! thou art a prize truly and indeed invaluable, for never canst thou be too dearly bought !"

As an improvement upon a street ditty Burns wrote

A RED, RED ROSE.

My Luve is like a red, red rose,
　　That 's newly sprung in June:
My Luve is like the melodie,
　　That 's sweetly play'd in tune.

As fair art thou, my bonie lass,
　　So deep in luve am I:
And I will luve thee still, my Dear,
　　Till a' the seas gang dry.

Till a' the seas gang dry, my Dear,
　　And the rocks melt wi' the sun;
And I will luve thee still, my Dear,
　　While the sands o' life shall run.

And fare-thee-well, my only Luve !
　　And fare-thee-well awhile !
And I will come again, my Luve,
　　Tho' 't were ten thousand mile !

It is worth while to remember Hazlitt's comment on this simple lyric, quoted above in connection with *Mary Morison.*

In 1795, when it was safer for a reformer to speak out
5 than it had been since 1792, Burns wrote Thomson: "A great critic, Aikin, on songs says that Love and Wine are the exclusive themes for song-writing. The following is on neither subject and consequently is no Song; but will be allowed, I think, to be two or three pretty good
10 *prose* thoughts inverted into rhyme":

A MAN'S A MAN FOR A' THAT.

Is there, for honest poverty,
 That hings his head, an' a' that?
The coward slave, we pass him by,
 We dare be poor for a' that!
15   For a' that, an' a' that,
   Our toils obscure, an' a' that;
   The rank is but the guinea's stamp;
   The man's the gowd[1] for a' that.

What tho' on hamely fare we dine,
20 Wear hodden-gray,[2] an' a' that;
Gie fools their silks, and knaves their wine,
 A man's a man for a' that.
  For a' that, an' a' that,
   Their tinsel show, an' a' that;
25   The honest man, tho' e'er sae poor,
   Is king o' men for a' that.

Ye see yon birkie,[3] ca'd a lord,
 Wha struts, an' stares, an' a' that;

---

[1] gold. [2] coarse woolen cloth. [3] fellow.

Tho' hundreds worship at his word,
　He 's but a coof [1] for a' that :
　　For a' that, an' a' that,
　　　His riband, star, an' a' that,
　　The man o' independent mind,
　　　He looks and laughs at a' that.　　5

A prince can mak a belted knight,
　A marquis, duke, an' a' that;
But an honest man 's aboon his might,
　Guid faith he mauna fa' [2] that !　　10
　　For a' that, an' a' that,
　　　Their dignities, an' a' that,
　　The pith o' sense, an' pride o' worth,
　　　Are higher rank than a' that.

Then let us pray that come it may,　　15
　As come it will for a' that,
That sense and worth, o'er a' the earth,
　May bear the gree,[3] an' a' that.
　　For a' that, an' a' that,
　　　It 's coming yet, for a' that,　　20
　　That man to man, the warld o'er,
　　　Shall brothers be for a' that.

"I do not give you the foregoing song for your book,
. . . for the piece is not really poetry."

Mr. Logie Robertson says : "If it be not poetry — and 25
Matthew Arnold of all critics alone agrees with the
author — it is something better." Whatever we call the
lyric, many a British heart responded to the sentiments,
and the spirit of it is worth considering in connection
with the American Revolution as well as with that of the 30

　　[1] fool.　　[2] must not claim.　　[3] prize.

French. "It is so characteristic of Burns," says Douglas, "that of all the poems and songs he ever wrote, it could be least spared from a collection of his works." What other song so effectively sings Liberty, Equality, Fraternity? It is good sense, good politics, good religion.

The next year was the poet's last. During his fatal illness he was attended by a kind-hearted friend of Mrs. Burns. One morning he suggested to this young woman that if she would like new verses to any favorite tune, he would do his best to produce some. She at once played a melody she liked until Burns became familiar with it, and a few minutes later he handed her these verses:

O, WERT THOU IN THE CAULD BLAST.

O, WERT thou in the cauld blast,
    On yonder lea, on yonder lea,
My plaidie to the angry airt,[1]
    I 'd shelter thee, I 'd shelter thee.
Or did misfortune's bitter storms
    Around thee blaw, around thee blaw,
Thy beild [2] should be my bosom,
    To share it a', to share it a'.

Or were I in the wildest waste,
    Sae black and bare, sae black and bare,
The desert were a paradise,
    If thou wert there, if thou wert there.
Or were I monarch o' the globe,
    Wi' thee to reign, wi' thee to reign,
The brightest jewel in my crown
    Wad be my queen, wad be my queen.

1 quarter.   2 shelter.

In this simple song the youthfulness of *Mary Morison* has developed into an expression of love that is mature and thoroughly refined. Much of the best poetry is incomplete until it is read aloud, but perhaps Mendelssohn has done more toward perfecting these two stanzas than the human voice can do, his melody harmonizes so exquisitely with the beautiful thought. It is with reverence that we listen as through the weird Scots atmosphere both the musician and the poet bring us the appealing message of one whose sympathy was enriched by suffering.

PRONUNCIATION.

[Mr. E. Charlton Black, of Cambridge, not only gave me valuable suggestions on this subject, but was thoughtful enough to read the manuscript to Dr. John Watson (Ian Maclaren).]

AFTER reminding us that the Scottish language is not a different language from English, but merely the northern dialect of English, Mr. John Stuart Blackie says : "The Scotch form of English bears on its face the distinct evidence of a dialect formed under the influence of music and popular minstrelsy. It is, philologically considered, the musical and lyrical variety of the general English speech, and as such has a claim to be recognized in the higher education of all who speak the common English tongue." Instead of giving it this recognition, however, we are likely to say with Robert Louis Stevenson that before long Burns's Ayrshire and Scott's "brave metropolitan utterance" will be "the ghosts of speech." Meantime let us not be timid about pronouncing this dying Scots-English. Inasmuch as every county has its peculiarities, hard and fast rules are out of place.

A has nearly the same variety of sounds that we have in the English *ale*, *care*, *arm*, *ask*, and *all*; *a'* is equivalent to *a* in *all*. *AI*, as in *mair*, is one way of indicating the sound of *a* in *care*. *E* is both short and long, much as in English. *I* generally has the sound of *i* in *bird* (sometimes it is like *i* in *pin*, or *u* in *cup*, occasionally like *i* in *fine*); *Y* has nearly

87

the same values. *O* has only one sound, as in *more;* whether long, as in *morn,* or short, as in *bonie,* the quality is practically the same. *U,* when not like *u* in *run,* or *oo* as in *moon,* is as much like the French *u* or German *ü* as it is like any one sound. *UI* and *OO,* as in *guid* and *aboon,* are but slight modifications of this sound. *OU* is like the English *oo.* *H,* when not silent, is strongly aspirate ; *r* rolls — sometimes into two syllables ; *ng* is simple, as in *lang-er* (not like the English *anger*) ; and *ch* and *gh* are strongly aspirated as gutturals, like the German *ch* after *a, o, u,* and *au.* E.g., *brought* is pronounced *brocht.* Final *ed* has the sound *et* or *it* and is sometimes so spelled. *-Ing* is pronounced like its ancient form *-and,* in which the *d* is silent.

INDEX OF TITLES AND FIRST LINES.

ESSAY ON BURNS

OUTLINE OF THE LIFE OF BURNS.

In the southwest corner of Scotland, on the coast, some thirty miles from Glasgow, is the little town of Ayr. It was in a two-roomed cottage near by that Robert Burns was born. He inherited from his strict, sturdy father a proud, quick temper; from his mother the love of song. Besides his birthplace, Burns had three other homes in Ayrshire, — Mount Oliphant, Lochlea, and Mossgiel.

Robert was a lad of seven when his father undertook to earn a living on the small upland farm of Mount Oliphant. He worked like a slave to do his part, as oldest boy, towards supporting the family. His regular attendance at school ended in his ninth year. After that he spent a few weeks at a time in several schools for some special purpose, but his principal teacher was his father. The one luxury that this wise father allowed himself was a library. Many books that he could not buy he would borrow; and in the gloom that enshrouds this life of incessant toil, which impaired permanently the physical and mental powers of the poet, there is certainly one bright spot. Although the Burns boys rarely saw anybody but their own family, they had in their father a companion who made it his business to educate his children. The fact must not be overlooked that Robert read, besides many other authors, Addison, Pope, Richardson, Smollett, Milton, and Shakspere. He was an eager and industrious reader. He absorbed much of the Bible, and of *A Select Collection of English Songs*, his *vade mecum*, he writes : "I pored over them driving my cart, or walking to labor, song by song, verse by verse — carefully noting the tender or sublime from affectation and fustian."

Into this monotonous life of drudgery and economy, brightened by the interesting reading and the profitable conversation that the worthy Scotsman so persistently introduced, came a new element; when in his fifteenth year Robert fell in love with the girl who was his partner in harvesting, and wrote "Handsome Nell," his first song. Later he wrote in his Commonplace Book, "I never had the least thought . . . of turning Poet till I got once heartily in Love, and then Rhyme and Song were, in a manner, the spontaneous language of my heart." Henceforth, as he himself said, this bit of tinder was "eternally lighted up by some Goddess or other."

After twelve years of patient toil in Mount Oliphant, the Burns family removed to Lochlea, in the parish of Tarbolton. Here they lived in a similar way, but more comfortably, during the following seven years. Robert made several variations in the routine of life. For a time he studied mensuration and surveying at Kirkoswald, a village full of smugglers and adventurers. Soon afterward he entered heartily into the founding and supporting of a debating society, the Bachelors' Club. According to his brother, he was in the secret of half the love affairs of the parish of Tarbolton, and was never without at least one of his own.

In his twenty-third year he tried, but in vain, to win the affections of a certain farmer's daughter. Much depressed, he then went to Irvine to learn flax-dressing. " In Irvine," writes his brother Gilbert, " he contracted some acquaintance of a freer manner of thinking and living than he had been used to, whose society prepared him for overleaping the bounds of rigid virtue which had hitherto restrained him. During this period, also, he became a Freemason, which was his first introduction to the life of a boon companion." But his melancholy grew on him, and his business venture proved a failure ; he returned to Lochlea, worked as hard as ever on the farm, and, if we may believe Gilbert, was frugal and temperate. He found time to be social and to write poems and songs.

His father had lived to see something of the poet's skill, but he died soon afterward, anxious lest the young man should prove lacking in will power.

Robert and Gilbert now leased the small farm of Mossgiel, near the village of Mauchline. In spite of the older son's determination and persistent efforts, the crops were a failure for two successive seasons, and the farmer lost heart. Yet, unfortunate as he was in his farming, undiscriminating and imprudent as he was in his wooing, he was so generous socially, and so frank to confess his follies that he had many friends among the worthy people of Ayrshire. The generous-hearted, upright Gavin Hamilton and the affectionate, cultured Robert Aiken encouraged, in many ways, the young poet who was industriously composing in the field and writing out at a deal table in the humble farmhouse a notable collection of verse. At Hamilton's suggestion, he published his first volume of poetry. There was no doubt that the author of this volume, although only twenty-six years old, was a genius.

This important event was quickly followed by another. The natural way for him to gain the attention of Scotland was by making himself known at Scotland's capital; so he went to Edinburgh. The reputation of the poet attracted the attention of the curious. The charm of the conversationalist held spellbound citizens of the highest rank. The pride and assurance of the Ayrshire plowman lent to his modesty and winsomeness a freedom and vigor that proved irresistibly fascinating. Naturally enough, in answer to the demand of his worshipers, a second edition of his poems was published within six months of his coming to the Scottish capital. In spite of all this flattering attention, Burns did not once lose his head.

During the summer and autumn he traveled in Scotland. After a Border tour, a brief visit with his family at Mossgiel, and three Highland tours, he returned to Edinburgh to spend the winter.

To one whose interest in the localities of Scottish song was so keen, the excursion must have been profitable in many ways, and it was altogether timely, for Burns had begun to specialize. He had tried his hand at satirical, descriptive, and lyrical verse. But now he was busily collecting material for the occupation on which he was to focus his energy in the future. Hitherto a poet, he was henceforth to be a singer.

About the second winter in Edinburgh there is little glamor. The aristocracy were not so hospitable, but Burns was prepared for their coolness. Whatever his friends might have done for him, had he asked assistance, it is to his credit that he accepted their freely offered aid in helping him to a farm and a position in the excise so gracefully that they seemed to think they were giving him what he was eager to get, instead of what he was patiently making up his mind to endure.

Burns was by no means unhappy when he married Jean Armour and settled down on the farm at Ellisland. As exciseman he had to ride some two hundred miles a week, and naturally people took pride in entertaining a guest at once so distinguished and so agreeable. After a stormy day's travel it must have been real recreation for the poet to doff his official dignity and enter heartily into the home life of friends, sometimes opening his whole soul in his artless way.

But his duties did not always keep the real man in the background. A diligent officer, severe with regular smugglers, he was merciful Robert Burns when he dealt with country brewers and retailers. He also took delight in working for the permanent good of his fellow-men. Long before there was any national movement in this direction, he set on foot a plan for the intellectual improvement of the community by taking an active part in establishing a public library. And while trying to do the work of two or three men, one day seizing a cargo of tobacco from an unlucky smuggler, the next punishing some poor wretch for selling liquor without a license, the same evening writing a beautiful poem, he did not lose sight of his high ideal of the mission of a poet. As in his Mossgiel days, he still "rhymed for fun"; he often wrote as a favor to a friend, but he could not bear the thought of writing for money.

During this period of hard work he had been buoyed up by the hope of promotion, but he found he must for the present give up the longed-for supervisorship and content himself with being an ordinary exciseman in Dumfries. Upon receiving the appointment, with a salary of seventy pounds, he gave up the farm, which had proved a losing investment, and in 1791 took a house of three rooms in this little town.

It was a time of revolution ; a time when quiet, pensive poets were stirred to their hearts' core. The excitement of the patriotic Burns, keenly sensitive to the welfare of Scotland, and especially of her peasants, at times knew no bounds. His sympathy for those who were trying to secure their rights through the French Revolution led to vigorous expressions of his ideas of liberty. Yet he was a government official. Loyal as he was, he was accused of disloyalty, and came very near losing his position. The tongue-tied poet felt keenly that the world was going wrong and that he was in no position to help right it. But the storm blew over; Burns afterwards took an active part in fighting for a Liberal in an election contest, and those friends who had carefully prevented the printing of many of his productions allowed the publication of several ballads that once would have been condemned.

There were intervals during this period in which he did almost no literary work. Much of his time was spent in helping Johnson make his collection of songs for his *Scots Musical Museum* and in contributing to Thomson's more ambitious and better edited work, the *Melodies of Scotland*. Meanwhile he was growing more melancholy. After settling in Dumfries the family lived in comparative comfort, yet toward the end of his life they were reduced to narrow straits. Outside of his home he had to encounter the contempt of the Dumfries aristocracy, but he recovered from their abuse and refused to part with his good humor. In his gloom he sought relief in " the merry song and the flowing bowl." At times he got real help and comfort and hope from religion. It was under such circumstances that he kept on writing songs.

Scotland had waited for her poet till the latter half of the eighteenth century — a long time. Even then he was destined to lead a life of incessant toil as a farmer and gauger, while his real work had to be done incidentally. His friends, recognizing his genius, had introduced him to Edinburgh, and so to Scotland ; he was becoming widely known, and was doing some of his best work, when, at the age of thirty-seven, he suddenly died.

OUTLINE OF THE LIFE OF CARLYLE.

Thomas Carlyle, born in 1795, seven months before Burns died, was the son of a frugal, undemonstrative father, a stone mason, and a worthy, intelligent mother. At their home in Ecclefechan his mother taught him to read, his father to count. In his seventh year the report came from the village school that he was "complete" in English. In 1809, after three years at a "doleful and hateful Academy," he began his five years' hermit course at Edinburgh University. He studied for the ministry, as his father wished, but could not conscientiously make that his life work. He says of this miserable period, "I was without friends, experience, or connection in the sphere of human business, was of sly humor, proud enough and to spare, and had begun my long curriculum of dyspepsia which has never ended since." The question was, what should he do for a living? The very difficulties in the way spurred him on to become a lawyer. To study law he needed money. To earn the money he taught school. But he could not tolerate the schoolmaster's drudgery, and gave up teaching; meanwhile he had studied law long enough to abandon it gladly on the ground that its miseries would lead to no reward but money.

At this point in his career Carlyle received substantial help from others. He owed much to a college friend, Edward Irving, who introduced him to Miss Jane Welsh, the witty, fascinating daughter of a country surgeon. The next year Irving helped him to some tutoring in London. He soon gave that up for literary work. Dyspepsia and "the noises" drove him from the metropolis to a little farm at Hoddam Hill. There he spent a quiet year making translations from the German. Forty years later he referred to it as "perhaps the most triumphantly important" of his life. "He was building up his character," says Mr. John Nichol, "and forming the opinions which, with few material changes, he long continued to hold." He found his skepticisms and his agonizing doubtings giving way to quiet, spontaneous communings with Nature.

After many wearisome attempts to obtain recognition he saw that his life work was to be literature. In 1826, at the age of thirty-one, he married Miss Welsh. They began housekeeping in a cottage at Comely Bank, Edinburgh. Mrs. Carlyle was so charming a hostess that she attracted to their home more than one literary friend. Among the most devoted was Jeffrey, the editor of the *Edinburgh Review*. Before the end of another year, Carlyle had made the beginning of a literary reputation. For no sympathy was the young, struggling writer more grateful than for the genuine admiration shown by Goethe, foremost genius of the age, who recognized him as "a moral force of great importance."

But so far he had made only a beginning. He received so little for his writings that, for the sake of economy and quiet, he retired to Craigenputtock. Here it was, fifteen miles from Dumfries, five from the nearest neighbor, in a farmhouse amidst the dreary moorland, that Carlyle wrote the *Essay on Burns*. It appeared in the *Edinburgh Review* in December, 1828. During his six years of Craigenputtock life, the monotony of which was relieved by Emerson's memorable visit and several months spent in London and

Edinburgh, he wrote most of his biographical and critical essays and *Sartor Resartus*.

His youth had been spent amid bleak surroundings under the care of parents whom he revered and loved. Then came the struggle to know himself and to determine his position in the universe. All this prepared the way for his life in London.

He went to London in 1834 with little fame, less money, and few friends. He had written the *French Revolution* and *Hero-Worship*, and had resorted to the ugly expedient of lecturing, before the tardy recognition of the value of his work insured him a living. He still worked industriously, producing literature that gave abundant evidence of his independence in politics and religion. Then came the death of his mother, who, and who only, says Froude, "had stood between him and the loneliness of which he had so often and so passionately complained."

He withdrew from the world more than ever for the "desperate dead-lift pull" with his great *History of Friedrich II.* The result of his painful struggles was a triumph recognized in Scotland, England, and Germany. His own countrymen eagerly elected him Lord Rector of Edinburgh. His unique address to the students excited unbounded enthusiasm. It was the proudest, most joyous day of his life. But in the midst of his triumph his wife died. Stunned by her sudden death, he realized for the first time what she had been to him. He entered without warning the saddest period of his life. His fame was secure, but it had come too late. He cared little for it now that he could not share it with her. Success and failure were empty sounds. Yet the last years have an interest of their own. He had always been benevolent, eager to help the working classes; and as his own affliction increased he became still more eager to aid those in distress. Nor was he himself neglected.   Painters, sculptors, literary men, and disciples were bent on preserving the fame of the venerable Chelsea Prophet.   Best of all, firm friends stood by him in his need and comforted him.   Clearly, he did not find age a " crown of thorns "; yet he was haunted by

> " To-morrow and to-morrow and to-morrow."

He died in February, 1881, at the age of eighty-five.   In accordance with his own wish, he was buried in Ecclefechan with his kindred, rather than in Westminster Abbey.

BURNS AND CARLYLE.

———◆———

We naturally ask why Carlyle should write an account of Burns. He was preëminently the man to do it. The two men had much in common. In the first place, they were Scotchmen; more than that, they were Lowlanders. Of peasant birth, they began life in insignificant hamlets, and were brought up under similar home influences. Both had fathers notable for their integrity and independence. Neither was much indebted to the schools for his early education, but both were helped and encouraged by far-seeing, ambitious parents. The lads enjoyed books and read eagerly and widely. So much for their boyhood.

Each had to fight for a place in the world. Carlyle struggled for several years to secure a meager competence. With all his hard work, Burns barely made a living. The following statement about Carlyle applies quite as well to Burns: He rose — " not by birth or favor, not on the ladder of any established profession, but only by the internal force that was in him — to the highest place as a modern man of letters."

Both were entertained at the Scottish capital, and both stood the test. Burns was not spoiled; Carlyle was bored. In his *Reminiscences*, the dyspeptic writes of the " effulgences of ' Edinburgh society,' big dinners, parties," that it all passed away as "an obliging pageant merely." In spite of it, Burns retained his sincerity, his "indisputable air of Truth"; in spite of it, too, Carlyle remained thoroughly genuine.

Toward mankind their attitudes were very different, but neither hesitated to say just what he thought of persons he did not like ; neither wasted any sympathy on the upper classes ; both urged them to remember that those under them were human and were to be treated as men. Yet neither derived entire satisfaction from his relations with his fellows. Both were often heavy-hearted. The melancholy of the one is as genuine as the melancholy of the other. Burns had the happy faculty of turning his into gayety, but Carlyle, with all his humor, could get only partial relief.

Both are said to have been lovable men. We know Burns must have been particularly lovable, and we may be interested in the testimony of an Aberdonian, who said, " I knew Carlyle, and I aver to you that his heart was as large and generous as his brain was powerful ; that he was essentially a most lovable man, and that there were depths of tenderness, kindliness, benevolence, and most delicate courtesy in him, with all his seeming ruggedness and stern-ness, such as I have found throughout my life rarely in any human being." Mr. Froude says that when we know him fully, we shall not love or admire him the less "because he had infirmities like the rest of us."

We recognize Burns as a natural poet. "The intensity of Carlyle's vision," says Mr. John Nichol, " was that of a born artist." He adds, " None of our poets, from Chaucer and Dunbar to Burns and Tennyson, have been more alive to the influences of external nature."

As men of genius, they have been grouped, not with the Miltons and the Shaksperes, but with those who are like " the wind-harp which answers to the breath that touches it, now low and sweet, now rising into wild swell or angry scream, as the strings are swept by some passing gust."

Burns was a prophet-poet. He saw and thought and spoke for the world. In the vigorous Scotch way, he " spoke out." Carlyle was a prophet. "The mission of the Hebrew prophet," says Mr. Macpherson, "was by passionate utterance to keep alive in the minds of his countrymen a deep, abiding sense of life's mystery, sacredness, and solemnity. What Isaiah did for his day Carlyle did for the moderns."

Such was the man, then, who helps us interpret Scotland's darling poet. Carlyle speaks for Scotland. His is the tender voice of the fond mother, who, though confident that her son,

> " Who lives immortal in the hearts of men,"

will never die, yet loves to tell us, her eyes now tearful, now glowing with a mother's pride, about her boy. All this so simply, so naturally, so heartily, with a pathos like Burns's own that softens beautifully the stern, rugged Carlyle.

It would be difficult to find two great men about whom there has been more difference of opinion. Carlyle has been called "about the most cantankerous Scotchman that ever maltreated the English tongue." Mr. Richard Garnett, on the other hand, says that Carlyle's supremacy as a literary genius is attested by the fact that he is one of the very few in whose hands language is wholly flexible and fusible, and adds, "Great and deathless writer as he was, he will be honored by posterity for his influence on human life rather than for his supremacy as a literary artist." As to this influence on human life, the dying witness of John Sterling was : " Towards England no man has been and done like you." And Froude once wrote : " Leaving out Goethe, Carlyle was indisputably the greatest man (if you measure greatness by the permanent effect he has and will produce on the minds of mankind) who has appeared in Europe for centuries. His character was as remarkable as his intellect. There has been no man at all, not Goethe himself, who in thought and action was so consistently true to his noblest instincts."

As for Burns, criticise him as severely as you please, some of his best poetry will live forever as pure poetry. Wordsworth is not the only one whom Burns has shown

> " How verse may build a princely throne
> On humble truth,"

and careless, even indifferent readers can hardly help feeling that in some of his work

> " the passion and the pain
> Of hearts that long have ceased to beat remain
> To throb in hearts that are, or are to be."

There was nothing half-hearted about him. If he was independent, he was so independent that "no man ever existed who could look down on him. They that looked into his eyes saw that they might look down the sky as easily." In striking contrast to this fearlessness was his sympathy,—Burns's sympathy, large, whole-souled, world-wide, enough for all mankind, with plenty to spare for every living thing, and a drop left over for the deil.

If at times he turned teacher, his teaching was sound, and so effective that it was not to be forgotten. To be sure, he used satire so vigorously that he shocked some of his readers. That was their fault, not Burns's; they needed the shaking up. But one cannot separate his satire from his humor, — his joyous, rollicking, irresistible humor. " His humor and his wit scorched into cinders whole hecatombs of hypocrites and knaves, and his name is one at which ' Holy Willies ' of all degrees and homicidal Dr. Hornbrooks, both with and without degrees, ought to tremble."

How naturally and fully these characteristics blend in Burns, — humor, wit, good sense, satire, independence, sympathy, — above all, sympathy!

He was a man who knew men and how to appeal to men. When he spoke to his neighbors, he spoke with a voice that men everywhere understood. He has been called provincial; he was also national and universal. And I care not how many are our expressions of admiration for his love of nature, his descriptions of scenery, his graphic power, his terse, lucid, forcible, often elegant style; back of the great artist we must see the sincere man in his own simple way dealing directly with human life.

His earlier work consisted largely of satires, descriptions of country life, and epistles. Afterward he drifted more and more into song-writing. It may be worth while to consider the question whether the miscellaneous poems show more clearly the greatness of the poet; but long after we have forgotten most of them, I fancy, we shall be singing the songs. Exactly why it may be hard to tell. He expresses beautifully what we know to be true. He sings tunefully what we have often felt. Other poets have done this for us; but there is something subtle about Burns's way of doing it. We sometimes feel that others have made an effort to speak for us and to please us. Somehow we get the impression that Burns's writing was as unstudied, as natural, as spontaneous as his breathing. Many of the songs seem to have written themselves, and we find ourselves singing them as if they were our own. Other poets we like and admire; to some extent we may make them ours — Burns in his own winning way charms us; before we know it, we are his.

BURNS.[1]

[1828.]

In the modern arrangements of society, it is no uncom-
mon thing that a man of genius must, like Butler, 'ask
for bread and receive a stone;' for, in spite of our grand
maxim of supply and demand, it is by no means the
highest excellence that men are most forward to recognise.   5.
The inventor of a spinning-jenny is pretty sure of his
reward in his own day; but the writer of a true poëm, like
the apostle of a true religion, is nearly as sure of the
contrary. We do not know whether it is not an aggra-
vation of the injustice, that there is generally a posthu-   10
mous retribution. Robert Burns, in the course of Nature,
might yet have been living; but his short life was spent
in toil and penury; and he died, in the prime of his manhood, miserable and neglected: and yet already a brave
mausoleum shines over his dust, and more than one   15
splendid monument has been reared in other places to
his fame; the street where he languished in poverty is
called by his name; the highest personages in our literature have been proud to appear as his commentators and
admirers; and here is the *sixth* narrative of his *Life* that   20
has been given to the world!

Mr. Lockhart thinks it necessary to apologise for this
new attempt on such a subject: but his readers, we
believe, will readily acquit him; or, at worst, will censure
only the performance of his task, not the choice of it.   25
The character of Burns, indeed, is a theme that cannot

[1] EDINBURGH REVIEW, No. 96. — *The Life of Robert Burns.* By
J. G. Lockhart, LL.B. Edinburgh, 1828.

easily become either trite or exhausted; and will probably
gain rather than lose in its dimensions by the distance to
which it is removed by Time. No man, it has been said,
is a hero to his valet; and this is probably true; but the
5 fault is at least as likely to be the valet's as the hero's.
For it is certain, that to the vulgar eye few things are
wonderful that are not distant. It is difficult for men to
believe that the man, the mere man whom they see, nay
perhaps painfully feel, toiling at their side through the
10 poor jostlings of existence, can be made of finer clay than
themselves. Suppose that some dining acquaintance of
Sir Thomas Lucy's, and neighbour of John a Combe's, had
snatched an hour or two from the preservation of his
game, and written us a Life of Shakspeare! What
15 dissertations should we not have had,—not on *Hamlet*
and *The Tempest*, but on the wool-trade, and deer-stealing,
and the libel and vagrant laws; and how the Poacher
became a Player; and how Sir Thomas and Mr. John had
Christian bowels, and did not push him to extremities!
20 In like manner, we believe, with respect to Burns, that
till the companions of his pilgrimage, the Honourable
Excise Commissioners, and the Gentlemen of the Caledonian Hunt, and the Dumfries Aristocracy, and all the
Squires and Earls, equally with the Ayr Writers, and the
25 New and Old Light Clergy, whom he had to do with
shall have become invisible in the darkness of the Past,
or visible only by light borrowed from *his* juxtaposition,
it will be difficult to measure him by any true standard,
or to estimate what he really was and did, in the
30 eighteenth century, for his country and the world. It
will be difficult, we say; but still a fair problem for
literary historians; and repeated attempts will give us
repeated approximations.

His former Biographers have done something, no

doubt, but by no means a great deal, to assist us. Dr. Currie and Mr. Walker, the principal of these writers, have both, we think, mistaken one essentially important thing: Their own and the world's true relation to their author, and the style in which it became such men to think and to speak of such a man. Dr. Currie loved the poet truly; more perhaps than he avowed to his readers, or even to himself; yet he everywhere introduces him with a certain patronising, apologetic air; as if the polite public might think it strange and half unwarrantable that he, a man of science, a scholar and gentleman, should do such honour to a rustic. In all this, however, we readily admit that his fault was not want of love, but weakness of faith; and regret that the first and kindest of all our poet's biographers should not have seen farther, or believed more boldly what he saw. Mr. Walker offends more deeply in the same kind: and both err alike in presenting us with a detached catalogue of his several supposed attributes, virtues and vices, instead of a delineation of the resulting character as a living unity. This, however, is not painting a portrait; but gauging the length and breadth of the several features, and jotting down their dimensions in arithmetical ciphers. Nay it is not so much as that: for we are yet to learn by what arts or instruments the mind *could* be so measured and gauged.

Mr. Lockhart, we are happy to say, has avoided both these errors. He uniformly treats Burns as the high and remarkable man the public voice has now pronounced him to be: and in delineating him, he has avoided the method of separate generalities, and rather sought for characteristic incidents, habits, actions, sayings; in a word, for aspects which exhibit the whole man, as he looked and lived among his fellows. The book accordingly, with all its deficiencies, gives more insight, we think, into the true character of Burns, than any prior biography: though, being written on the very popular and condensed scheme of an article for *Constable's Miscellany*, it has less depth than we could have wished and expected from a writer of such power; and contains rather more, and more multifarious quotations than belong of right to an original production. Indeed, Mr. Lockhart's own writing is generally so good, so clear, direct and nervous, that we seldom wish to see it making place for another man's. However, the spirit of the work is throughout candid, tolerant and anxiously conciliating; compliments and praises are liberally distributed, on all hands, to great and small; and, as Mr. Morris Birkbeck observes of the society in the backwoods of America, 'the courtesies of polite life are never lost sight of for a moment.' But there are better things than these in the volume; and we can safely testify, not only that it is easily and pleasantly read a first time, but may even be without difficulty read again.

Nevertheless, we are far from thinking that the problem of Burns's Biography has yet been adequately solved. We do not allude so much to deficiency of facts or documents, — though of these we are still every day receiving some fresh accession, — as to the limited and imperfect application of them to the great end of Biography. Our notions upon this subject may perhaps appear extravagant; but if an individual is really of consequence enough to have his life and character recorded for public remembrance, we have always been of opinion that the public ought to be made acquainted with all the inward springs and relations of his character. How did the world and man's life, from his particular position, represent themselves to his mind? How did coexisting circumstances modify him from without;

how did he modify these from within? With what endeavours and what efficacy rule over them; with
what resistance and what suffering sink under them?
In one word, what and how produced was the effect of
society on him; what and how produced was his effect
on society? He who should answer these questions, in
regard to any individual, would, as we believe, furnish a
model of perfection in Biography. Few individuals, indeed, can deserve such a study; and many *lives* will be
written, and, for the gratification of innocent curiosity,
ought to be written, and read and forgotten, which are
not in this sense *biographies*. But Burns, if we mistake
not, is one of these few individuals; and such a study,
at least with such a result, he has not yet obtained.
Our own contributions to it, we are aware, can be but
scanty and feeble; but we offer them with good-will,
and trust they may meet with acceptance from those they
are intended for.

Burns first came upon the world as a prodigy; and
was, in that character, entertained by it, in the usual
fashion, with loud, vague, tumultuous wonder, speedily
subsiding into censure and neglect; till his early and
most mournful death again awakened an enthusiasm for
him, which, especially as there was now nothing to be
done, and much to be spoken, has prolonged itself even
to our own time. It is true, the 'nine days' have long
since elapsed; and the very continuance of this clamour
proves that Burns was no vulgar wonder. Accordingly,
even in sober judgments, where, as years passed by, he
has come to rest more and more exclusively on his own
intrinsic merits, and may now be well-nigh shorn of that
casual radiance, he appears not only as a true British
poet, but as one of the most considerable British men of

the eighteenth century. Let it not be objected that he
did little. He did much, if we consider where and how.
If the work performed was small, we must remember
that he had his very materials to discover; for the metal
5 he worked in lay hid under the desert moor, where no eye
but his had guessed its existence; and we may almost
say, that with his own hand he had to construct the tools
for fashioning it. For he found himself in deepest obscurity, without help, without instruction, without model;
10 or with models only of the meanest sort. An educated man stands, as it were, in the midst of a boundless
arsenal and magazine, filled with all the weapons and
engines which man's skill has been able to devise from
the earliest time; and he works, accordingly, with a
15 strength borrowed from all past ages. How different is
his state who stands on the outside of that storehouse,
and feels that its gates must be stormed, or remain forever shut against him ! His means are the commonest
and rudest; the mere work done is no measure of his
20 strength. A dwarf behind his steam-engine may remove
mountains; but no dwarf will hew them down with a
pickaxe; and he must be a Titan that hurls them abroad
with his arms.

It is in this last shape that Burns presents himself.
25 Born in an age the most prosaic Britain had yet seen,
and in a condition the most disadvantageous, where his
mind, if it accomplished aught, must accomplish it under
the pressure of continual bodily toil, nay of penury and
desponding apprehension of the worst evils, and with no
30 furtherance but such knowledge as dwells in a poor
man's hut, and the rhymes of a Ferguson or Ramsay for
his standard of beauty, he sinks not under all these im-
pediments: through the fogs and darkness of that obscure
region, his lynx eye discerns the true relations of the

world and human life; he grows into intellectual strength, and trains himself into intellectual expertness. Impelled by the expansive movement of his own irrepressible soul, he struggles forward into the general view; and with haughty modesty lays down before us, as the fruit of his labour, a gift, which Time has now pronounced imperishable. Add to all this, that his darksome drudging childhood and youth was by far the kindliest era of his whole life; and that he died in his thirty-seventh year: and then ask, If it be strange that his poems are imperfect, and of small extent, or that his genius attained no mastery in its art? Alas, his Sun shone as through a tropical tornado; and the pale Shadow of Death eclipsed it at noon! Shrouded in such baleful vapours, the genius of Burns was never seen in clear azure splendour, enlightening the world: but some beams from it did, by fits, pierce through; and it tinted those clouds with rainbow and orient colours, into a glory and stern grandeur, which men silently gazed on with wonder and tears !

We are anxious not to exaggerate; for it is exposition rather than admiration that our readers require of us here ; and yet to avoid some tendency to that side is no easy matter. We love Burns, and we pity him ; and love and pity are prone to magnify. Criticism, it is sometimes thought, should be a cold business ; we are not so sure of this ; but, at all events, our concern with Burns is not exclusively that of critics. True and genial as his poetry must appear, it is not chiefly as a poet, but as a man, that he interests and affects us. He was often advised to write a tragedy : time and means were not lent him for this ; but through life he enacted a tragedy, and one of the deepest. We question whether the world has since witnessed so utterly sad a scene;

whether Napoleon himself, left to brawl with Sir Hudson Lowe, and perish on his rock, 'amid the melancholy main,' presented to the reflecting mind such a 'spectacle of pity and fear' as did this intrinsically nobler, gentler and perhaps greater soul, wasting itself away in a hopeless struggle with base entanglements which coiled closer and closer round him, till only death opened him an outlet. Conquerors are a class of men with whom, for most part, the world could well dispense; nor can the hard intellect, the unsympathising loftiness and high but selfish enthusiasm of such persons inspire us in general with any affection; at best it may excite amazement; and their fall, like that of a pyramid, will be beheld with a certain sadness and awe. But a true Poet, a man in whose heart resides some effluence of Wisdom, some tone of the 'Eternal Melodies,' is the most precious gift that can be bestowed on a generation: we see in him a freer, purer development of whatever is noblest in ourselves; his life is a rich lesson to us; and we mourn his death as that of a benefactor who loved and taught us.

Such a gift had Nature, in her bounty, bestowed on us in Robert Burns; but with queenlike indifference she cast it from her hand, like a thing of no moment; and it was defaced and torn asunder, as an idle bauble, before we recognised it. To the ill-starred Burns was given the power of making man's life more venerable, but that of wisely guiding his own life was not given. Destiny, — for so in our ignorance we must speak, — his faults, the faults of others, proved too hard for him; and that spirit, which might have soared could it but have walked, soon sank to the dust, its glorious faculties trodden under foot in the blossom; and died, we may almost say, without ever having lived. And so kind and warm a soul; so full of inborn riches, of love to all living and lifeless things! How his heart flows out in sympathy over universal Nature; and in her bleakest provinces discerns a beauty and a meaning! The 'Daisy' falls not unheeded under his ploughshare; nor the ruined nest of that 'wee, cowering, timorous beastie,' cast forth, after all its provident pains, to 'thole [1] the sleety dribble and cranreuch [2] cauld.' The 'hoar visage' of Winter delights him; he dwells with a sad and oft-returning fondness in these scenes of solemn desolation; but the voice of the tempest becomes an anthem to his ears; he loves to walk in the sounding woods, for 'it raises his thoughts to *Him that walketh on the wings of the wind.*' A true Poet-soul, for it needs but to be struck, and the sound it yields will be music! But observe him chiefly as he mingles with his brother men. What warm, all-comprehending fellow-feeling; what trustful, boundless love; what generous exaggeration of the object loved! His rustic friend, his nut-brown maiden, are no longer mean and homely, but a hero and a queen, whom he prizes as the paragons of Earth. The rough scenes of Scottish life, not seen by him in any Arcadian illusion, but in the rude contradiction, in the smoke and soil of a too harsh reality, are still lovely to him: Poverty is indeed his companion, but Love also, and Courage; the simple feelings, the worth, the nobleness, that dwell under the straw roof, are dear and venerable to his heart: and thus over the lowest provinces of man's existence he pours the glory of his own soul; and they rise, in shadow and sunshine, softened and brightened into a beauty which other eyes discern not in the highest. He has a just self-consciousness, which too often degenerates into pride; yet it is a noble pride, for

---

[1] Endure.   [2] Hoarfrost.

defence, not for offence; no cold suspicious feeling, but
a frank and social one. The Peasant Poet bears himself, we might say, like a King in exile: he is cast among
the low, and feels himself equal to the highest; yet he
5 claims no rank, that none may be disputed to him. The
forward he can repel, the supercilious he can subdue;
pretensions of wealth or ancestry are of no avail with
him; there is a fire in that dark eye, under which the
'insolence of condescension' cannot thrive. In his
10 abasement, in his extreme need, he forgets not for a
moment the majesty of Poetry and Manhood. And yet,
far as he feels himself above common men, he wanders
not apart from them, but mixes warmly in their interests;
nay throws himself into their arms, and, as it were,
15 entreats them to love him. It is moving to see how, in
his darkest despondency, this proud being still seeks
relief from friendship; unbosoms himself often to the
unworthy; and, amid tears, strains to his glowing heart a
heart that knows only the name of friendship. And yet
20 he was 'quick to learn'; a man of keen vision, before
whom common disguises afforded no concealment. His
understanding saw through the hollowness even of accomplished deceivers; but there was a generous credulity in
his heart. And so did our Peasant show himself among
25 us; 'a soul like an Æolian harp, in whose strings the
vulgar wind, as it passed through them, changed itself into
articulate melody.' And this was he for whom the world
found no fitter business than quarrelling with smugglers
and vintners, computing excise-dues upon tallow, and
30 gauging ale barrels! In such toils was that mighty
Spirit sorrowfully wasted: and a hundred years may pass
on before another such is given us to waste.

All that remains of Burns, the Writings he has left,

seem to us, as we hinted above, no more than a poor mutilated fraction of what was in him; brief, broken glimpses of a genius that could never show itself complete; that wanted all things for completeness: culture, leisure, true effort, nay even length of life. His poems are, with scarcely any exception, mere occasional effusions; poured forth with little premeditation; expressing, by such means as offered, the passion, opinion, or humour of the hour. Never in one instance was it permitted him to grapple with any subject with the full collection of his strength, to fuse and mould it in the concentrated fire of his genius. To try by the strict rules of Art such imperfect fragments, would be at once unprofitable and unfair. Nevertheless, there is something in these poems, marred and defective as they are, which forbids the most fastidious student of poetry to pass them by. Some sort of enduring quality they must have: for after fifty years of the wildest vicissitudes in poetic taste, they still continue to be read; nay, are read more and more eagerly, more and more extensively; and this not only by literary virtuosos, and that class upon whom transitory causes operate most strongly, but by all classes, down to the most hard, unlettered and truly natural class, who read little, and especially no poetry, except because they find pleasure in it. The grounds of so singular and wide a popularity, which extends, in a literal sense, from the palace to the hut, and over all regions where the English tongue is spoken, are well worth inquiring into. After every just deduction, it seems to imply some rare excellence in these works. What is that excellence?

To answer this question will not lead us far. The excellence of Burns is, indeed, among the rarest, whether in poetry or prose; but, at the same time, it is plain and easily recognised: his *Sincerity*, his indisput-

able air of Truth. Here are no fabulous woes or joys;
no hollow fantastic sentimentalities; no wiredrawn refin-
ings, either in thought or feeling: the passion that is
traced before us has glowed in a living heart; the opin-
5 ion he utters has risen in his own understanding, and
been a light to his own steps. He does not write from
hearsay, but from sight and experience; it is the scenes
that he has lived and laboured amidst, that he describes:
those scenes, rude and humble as they are, have kindled
10 beautiful emotions in his soul, noble thoughts, and definite resolves; and he speaks forth what is in him, not
from any outward call of vanity or interest, but because
his heart is too full to be silent. He speaks it with such
melody and modulation as he can; 'in homely rustic
15 jingle;' but it is his own, and genuine. This is the grand
secret for finding readers and retaining them: let him
who would move and convince others, be first moved and
convinced himself. Horace's rule, *Si vis me flere*, is
applicable in a wider sense than the literal one. To every
20 poet, to every writer, we might say: Be true, if you
would be believed. Let a man but speak forth with
genuine earnestness the thought, the emotion, the actual
condition of his own heart; and other men, so strangely
are we all knit together by the tie of sympathy, must and
25 will give heed to him. In culture, in extent of view, we
may stand above the speaker, or below him; but in
either case, his words, if they are earnest and sincere,
will find some response within us; for in spite of all
casual varieties in outward rank or inward, as face
30 answers to face, so does the heart of man to man.

This may appear a very simple principle, and one
which Burns had little merit in discovering. True, the
discovery is easy enough: but the practical appliance is
not easy; is indeed the fundamental difficulty which all

poets have to strive with, and which scarcely one in the
hundred ever fairly surmounts. (A head too dull to dis-
criminate the true from the false; a heart too dull to love
the one at all risks, and to hate the other in spite of all
temptations, are alike fatal to a writer.) With either, or as 5
more commonly happens, with both of these deficiencies
combine a love of distinction, a wish to be original, which
is seldom wanting, and we have Affectation, the bane of
literature, as Cant, its elder brother, is of morals. How
often does the one and the other front us, in poetry, as in 10
life! Great poets themselves are not always free of this
vice; nay, it is precisely on a certain sort and degree of
greatness that it is most commonly ingrafted. A strong
effort after excellence will sometimes solace itself with a
mere shadow of success; he who has much to unfold, will 15
sometimes unfold it imperfectly. Byron, for instance,
was no common man: yet if we examine his poetry with
this view, we shall find it far enough from faultless.
Generally speaking, we should say that it is not true.
He refreshes us, not with the divine fountain, but too 20
often with vulgar strong waters, stimulating indeed to
the taste, but soon ending in dislike, or even nausea.
Are his Harolds and Giaours, we would ask, real men;
we mean, poetically consistent and conceivable men? Do
not these characters, does not the character of their 25
author, which more or less shines through them all, rather
appear a thing put on for the occasion; no natural or
possible mode of being, but something intended to look
much grander than nature? Surely, all these stormful
agonies, this volcanic heroism, superhuman contempt and 30
moody desperation, with so much scowling, and teeth-
gnashing, and other sulphurous humour, is more like the
brawling of a player in some paltry tragedy, which is to
last three hours, than the bearing of a man in the busi-

ness of life, which is to last threescore and ten years.
To our minds there is a taint of this sort, something which
we should call theatrical, false, affected, in every one of
these otherwise so powerful pieces.   Perhaps *Don Juan*,
especially the latter parts of it, is the only thing approach-
ing to a *sincere* work, he ever wrote ; the only work where
he showed himself, in any measure, as he was; and
seemed so intent on his subject as, for moments, to forget himself.   Yet Byron hated this vice; we believe,
heartily detested it : nay he had declared formal war
against it in words.   So difficult is it even for the strongest to make this primary attainment, which might seem
the simplest of all: to *read its own consciousness without
mistakes*, without errors involuntary or wilful !   We recollect no poet of Burns's susceptibility who comes before us
from the first, and abides with us to the last, with such a
total want of affection.   He is an honest man, and an
honest writer.   In his successes and his failures, in his
greatness and his littleness, he is ever clear, simple, true,
and glitters with no lustre but his own.   We reckon this
to be a great virtue; to be, in fact, the root of most
other virtues, literary as well as moral.

Here, however, let us say, it is to the Poetry of Burns
that we now allude; to those writings which he had time
to meditate, and where no special reason existed to warp
his critical feeling, or obstruct his endeavour to fulfil it.
Certain of his Letters, and other fractions of prose composition, by no means deserve this praise.   Here, doubtless, there is not the same natural truth of style; but, on
the contrary, something not only stiff, but strained and
twisted ; a certain high-flown inflated tone; the stilting
emphasis of which contrasts ill with the firmness and
rugged simplicity of even his poorest verses.   Thus no
man, it would appear, is altogether unaffected.   Does not

Shakspeare himself sometimes premeditate the sheerest bombast ! But even with regard to these Letters of Burns, it is but fair to state that he had two excuses. The first was his comparative deficiency in language. Burns, though for most part he writes with singular force and even gracefulness, is not master of English prose, as he is of Scottish verse; not master of it, we mean, in proportion to the depth and vehemence of his matter. These Letters strike us as the effort of a man to express something which he has no organ fit for expressing. But a second and weightier excuse is to be found in the peculiarity of Burns's social rank. His correspondents are often men whose relation to him he has never accurately ascertained; whom therefore he is either forearming himself against, or else unconsciously flattering, by adopting the style he thinks will please them. At all events, we should remember that these faults, even in his Letters, are not the rule, but the exception. Whenever he writes, as one would ever wish to do, to trusted friends and on real interests, his style becomes simple, vigorous, expressive, sometimes even beautiful. His letters to Mrs. Dunlop are uniformly excellent.

But we return to his Poetry. In addition to its Sincerity, it has another peculiar merit, which indeed is but a mode, or perhaps a means, of the foregoing : this displays itself in his choice of subjects; or rather in his indifference as to subjects, and the power he has of making all subjects interesting. The ordinary poet, like the ordinary man, is forever seeking in external circumstances the help which can be found only in himself. In what is familiar and near at hand, he discerns no form or comeliness: home is not poetical, but prosaic; it is in some past, distant, conventional heroic world that poetry resides. Were he there and not here, were he thus and not so, it would be well with him. Hence our innumerable host of rose-coloured Novels and iron-mailed Epics, with their locality not on the Earth, but somewhere nearer to the Moon. Hence our Virgins of the Sun, and 5 our Knights of the Cross, malicious Saracens in turbans, and copper-coloured Chiefs in wampum, and so many other truculent figures from the heroic times or the heroic climates, who on all hands swarm in our poetry. Peace be with them ! But yet, as a great moralist proposed 10 preaching to the men of this century, so would we fain preach to the poets, 'a sermon on the duty of staying at home.' Let them be sure that heroic ages and heroic climates can do little for them. That form of life has attraction for us, less because it is better or nobler than 15 our own, than simply because it is different; and even this attraction must be of the most transient sort. For will not our own age, one day, be an ancient one; and have as quaint a costume as the rest; not contrasted with the rest, therefore, but ranked along with them in 20 respect of quaintness? Does Homer interest us now, because he wrote of what passed beyond his native Greece, and two centuries before he was born; or because he wrote what passed in God's world, and in the heart of man, which is the same after thirty centuries ? Let our 25 poets look to this : is their feeling really finer, truer, and their vision deeper than that of other men,— they have nothing to fear, even from the humblest subject; is it not so,— they have nothing to hope, but an ephemeral favour, even from the highest. 30 The poet, we imagine, can never have far to seek for a subject : the elements of his art are in him, and around him on every hand; for him the Ideal world is not remote from the Actual, but under it and within it : nay, he is a poet, precisely because he can discern it there. Wher-

ever there is a sky above him, and a world around him,
the poet is in his place; for here too is man's existence,
with its infinite longings and small acquirings; its ever-
thwarted, ever-renewed endeavours; its unspeakable
aspirations, its fears and hopes that wander through   5
Eternity; and all the mystery of brightness and of gloom
that it was ever made of, in any age or climate, since
man first began to live. Is there not the fifth act of a
Tragedy in every death-bed, though it were a peasant's,
and a bed of heath? And are wooings and weddings   10
obsolete, that there can be Comedy no longer! Or are
men suddenly grown wise, that Laughter must no longer
shake his sides, but be cheated of his Farce? Man's life
and nature is, as it was, and as it will ever be. But the
poet must have an eye to read these things, and a heart   15
to understand them; or they come and pass away before
him in vain. He is a *vates*, a seer; a gift of vision has
been given him. Has life no meanings for him, which
another cannot equally decipher; then he is no poet,
and Delphi itself will not make him one.   20

In this respect, Burns, though not perhaps absolutely
a great poet, better manifests his capability, better proves
the truth of his genius, than if he had by his own strength
kept the whole Minerva Press going to the end of his
literary course. He shows himself at least a poet of   25
Nature's own making; and Nature, after all, is still the
grand agent in making poets. We often hear of this and
the other external condition being requisite for the existence of a poet. Sometimes it is a certain sort of training;
he must have studied certain things, studied for instance   30
'the elder dramatists,' and so learned a poetic language;
as if poetry lay in the tongue, not in the heart. At other
times we are told he must be bred in a certain rank, and
must be on a confidential footing with the higher classes;

because, above all things, he must see the world. As to seeing the world, we apprehend this will cause him little difficulty, if he have but eyesight to see it with. Without eyesight, indeed, the task might be hard. The blind or the purblind man 'travels from Dan to Beersheba, and finds it all barren.' But happily every poet is born *in* the world ; and sees it, with or against his will, every day and every hour he lives. The mysterious workmanship of man's heart, the true light and the inscrutable darkness of man's destiny, reveal themselves not only in capital cities and crowded saloons, but in every hut and hamlet where men have their abode. Nay, do not the elements of all human virtues and all human vices; the passions at once of a Borgia and of a Luther, lie written, in stronger or fainter lines, in the consciousness of every individual bosom, that has practised honest self-examination? Truly, this same world may be seen in Mossgiel and Tarbolton, if we look well, as clearly as it ever came to light in Crockford's or the Tuileries itself.

But sometimes still harder requisitions are laid on the poor aspirant to poetry; for it is hinted that he should have *been born* two centuries ago; inasmuch as poetry, about that date, vanished from the earth, and became no longer attainable by men! Such cobweb speculations have, now and then, overhung the field of literature; but they obstruct not the growth of any plant there: the Shakspeare or the Burns, unconsciously and merely as he walks onward, silently brushes them away. Is not every genius an impossibility till he appear? Why do we call him new and original, if *we* saw where his marble was lying, and what fabric he could rear from it? It is not the material but the workman that is wanting. It is not the dark *place* that hinders, but the dim *eye*. A Scottish peasant's life was the meanest and rudest of all lives, till

Burns became a poet in it, and a poet of it; found it a *man's* life, and therefore significant to men. A thousand battle-fields remain unsung; but the *Wounded Hare* has not perished without its memorial; a balm of mercy yet breathes on us from its dumb agonies, because a poet was there. 5 Our *Halloween* had passed and repassed, in rude awe and laughter, since the era of the Druids; but no Theocritus, till Burns, discerned in it the materials of a Scottish Idyl: neither was the *Holy Fair* any *Council of Trent* or Roman *Jubilee;* but nevertheless, *Superstition* and *Hypocrisy* and 10 *Fun* having been propitious to him, in this man's hand it became a poem, instinct with satire and genuine comic life. Let but the true poet be given us, we repeat it, place him where and how you will, and true poetry will not be wanting.

Independently of the essential gift of poetic feeling, as 15 we have now attempted to describe it, a certain rugged sterling worth pervades whatever Burns has written; a virtue, as of green fields and mountain breezes, dwells in his poetry; it is redolent of natural life and hardy natural men. There is a decisive strength in him, and yet a 20 sweet native gracefulness: he is tender, he is vehement, yet without constraint or too visible effort; he melts the heart, or inflames it, with a power which seems habitual and familiar to him. We see that in this man there was the gentleness, the trembling pity of a woman, with the 25 deep earnestness, the force and passionate ardour of a hero. Tears lie in him, and consuming fire; as light-ning lurks in the drops of the summer cloud. He has a resonance in his bosom for every note of human feeling; the high and the low, the sad, the ludicrous, the joyful, 30 are welcome in their turns to his 'lightly-moved and all-conceiving spirit.' And observe with what a fierce prompt force he grasps his subject, be it what it may! How he fixes, as it were, the full image of the matter in

his eye; full and clear in every lineament; and catches the
real type and essence of it, amid a thousand accidents and
superficial circumstances, no one of which misleads him!
Is it of reason; some truth to be discovered? No sophistry,
5 no vain surface-logic detains him; quick, resolute, unerring,
he pierces through into the marrow of the question; and
speaks his verdict with an emphasis that cannot be forgotten.
Is it of description; some visual object to be represented?
No poet of any age or nation is more graphic than Burns:
10 the characteristic features disclose themselves to him at a
glance; three lines from his hand, and we have a likeness.
And, in that rough dialect, in that rude, often awkward
metre, so clear and definite a likeness! It seems a
draughtsman working with a burnt stick; and yet the
15 burin of a Retzsch is not more expressive or exact.

Of this last excellence, the plainest and most comprehensive of all, being indeed the root and foundation of
every sort of talent, poetical or intellectual, we could produce innumerable instances from the writings of Burns.
20 Take these glimpses of a snow-storm from his *Winter
Night* (the italics are ours):

> When biting Boreas, fell and doure,[1]
> *Sharp shivers* thro' the leafless bow'r,
> And Phœbus *gies a short-liv'd glowr*
>   *Far south the lift,*[2]
25 > *Dim-dark'ning thro' the flaky show'r*
>   *Or whirling drift:*
>
> 'Ae night the storm the steeples rock'd,
> Poor labour sweet in sleep was lock'd,
30 > While burns *wi' snawy wreeths upchok'd*
>   *Wild-eddying swirl,*
> Or thro' the mining outlet bock'd[3]
>   Down headlong hurl.

[1] Keen and stubborn.   [2] Sky.   [3] Gushed.

Are there not 'descriptive touches' here? The describer *saw* this thing; the essential feature and true likeness of every circumstance in it; saw, and not with the eye only. 'Poor labour locked in sweet sleep;' the dead stillness of man, unconscious, vanquished, yet not unprotected, while such strife of the material elements rages, and seems to reign supreme in loneliness : this is of the heart as well as of the eye ! — Look also at his image of a thaw, and prophesied fall of the *Auld Brig:*

> When heavy, dark, continued, a'-day rains
> Wi' deepening deluges o'erflow the plains ;
> When from the hills where springs the brawling Coil,
> Or stately Lugar's *mossy* fountains *boil,*
> Or where the Greenock winds his *moorland* course,
> Or haunted Garpal[1] draws his feeble source,
> Arous'd by blust'ring winds and *spotting* thowes,[2]
> *In mony a torrent down his snaw-broo rowes;*[3]
> *While crashing ice, borne on the roaring speat,*[4]
> *Sweeps dams and mills and brigs*[5] *a' to the gate;*
> And from Glenbuck down to the Rottenkey,
> Auld Ayr is just one lengthen'd *tumbling* sea ;
> Then down ye'll hurl, Deil nor ye never rise !
> And *dash the gumlie jaups*[6] *up to the pouring skies.*

The last line is in itself a Poussin-picture of that Deluge ! The welkin has, as it were, bent down with its weight; the 'gumlie jaups' and the 'pouring skies' are mingled together ; it is a world of rain and ruin. In respect of mere clearness and minute fidelity, the *Farmer's* commendation of his *Auld Mare,* in plough or in cart, may vie with Homer's Smithy of the Cyclops, or yoking of Priam's Chariot. Nor have we forgotten stout *Burn-*

---

[1] *Fabulosus* Hydaspes ! *C.*   [2] Thaws.   [3] Melted snow rolls.
[4] A flood after heavy rain, or thaw.
[5] Bridges.   [6] Splashes of muddy water.

the-wind [1] and his brawny customers, inspired by *Scotch Drink:* but it is needless to multiply examples. One other trait of a much finer sort we select from multitudes of such among his *Songs.* It gives, in a single line, to
5 the saddest feeling the saddest environment and local habitation :

> *The pale Moon is setting beyond the white wave,*
> *And Time is setting wi' me, O ;*
> Farewell, false friends ! false lover, farewell !
10 I 'll nae mair trouble them nor thee, O.

This clearness of sight we have called the foundation of all talent ; for in fact, unless we *see* our object, how shall we know how to place or prize it; in our understanding, our imagination, our affections? Yet it is not
15 in itself, perhaps, a very high excellence ; but capable of being united indifferently with the strongest, or with ordinary power. Homer surpasses all men in this quality : but strangely enough, at no great distance below him are Richardson and Defoe. It belongs, in
20 truth, to what is called a lively mind; and gives no sure indication of the higher endowments that may exist along with it. In all the three cases we have mentioned, it is combined with great garrulity ; their descriptions are detailed, ample and lovingly exact; Homer's fire bursts
25 through, from time to time, as if by accident; but Defoe and Richardson have no fire. Burns, again, is not more distinguished by the clearness than by the impetuous force of his conceptions. Of the strength, the piercing emphasis with which he thought, his emphasis of expres-
30 sion may give a humble but the readiest proof. Who ever uttered sharper sayings than his ; words more mem-

---

[1] A blacksmith.

orable, now by their burning vehemence, now by their
cool vigour and laconic pith ? A single phrase depicts
a whole subject, a whole scene. We hear of 'a gentleman that derived his patent of nobility direct from
Almighty God.' Our Scottish forefathers in the battle-
field struggled forward '*red-wat-shod*': in this one word,
a full vision of horror and carnage, perhaps too fright-
fully accurate for Art !

In fact, one of the leading features in the mind of
Burns is this vigour of his strictly intellectual percep-
tions. A resolute force is ever visible in his judgments,
and in his feelings and volitions. Professor Stewart
says of him, with some surprise: 'All the faculties of
Burns's mind were, as far as I could judge, equally
vigorous; and his predilection for poetry was rather the
result of his own enthusiastic and impassioned temper,
than of a genius exclusively adapted to that species of
composition. From his conversation I should have pronounced him to be fitted to excel in whatever walk of
ambition he had chosen to exert his abilities.' But this,
if we mistake not, is at all times the very essence of a
truly poetical endowment. Poetry, except in such cases
as that of Keats, where the whole consists in a weak-
eyed maudlin sensibility, and a certain vague random
tunefulness of nature, is no separate faculty, no organ
which can be superadded to the rest, or disjoined from
them; but rather the result of their general harmony and
completion. The feelings, the gifts that exist in the Poet
are those that exist, with more or less development, in
every human soul : the imagination, which shudders at
the Hell of Dante, is the same faculty, weaker in
degree, which called that picture into being. How does
the Poet speak to men, with power, but by being still
more a man than they ? Shakspeare, it has been well

observed, in the planning and completing of his trage-
dies, has shown an Understanding, were it nothing more,
which might have governed states, or indited a *Novum
Organum.* What Burns's force of understanding may
5 have been, we have less means of judging : it had to
dwell among the humblest objects ; never saw Philosophy ; never rose, except by natural effort and for short
intervals, into the region of great ideas. Nevertheless,
sufficient indication, if no proof sufficient, remains for
10 us in his works : we discern the brawny movements of a
gigantic though untutored strength ; and can understand
how, in conversation, his quick sure insight into men and
things may, as much as aught else about him, have
amazed the best thinkers of his time and country.

15   But, unless we mistake, the intellectual gift of Burns
is fine as well as strong. The more delicate relations of
things could not well have escaped his eye, for they were
intimately present to his heart. The logic of the senate
and the forum is indispensable, but not all-sufficient ;
20 nay perhaps the highest Truth is that which will the
most certainly elude it. For this logic works by words,
and 'the highest,' it has been said, 'cannot be expressed
in words.' We are not without tokens of an openness for
this higher truth also, of a keen though uncultivated
25 sense for it, having existed in Burns. Mr. Stewart, it
will be remembered, 'wonders,' in the passage above
quoted, that Burns had formed some distinct conception
of the 'doctrine of association.' We rather think that far
subtler things than the doctrine of association had from
30 of old been familiar to him. Here, for instance :

'We know nothing,' thus writes he, 'or next to nothing, of
the structure of our souls, so we cannot account for those seeming caprices in them, that one should be particularly pleased
with this thing, or struck with that, which, on minds of a

different cast, makes no extraordinary impression. I have some favourite flowers in spring, among which are the mountain-daisy, the harebell, the foxglove, the wild brier rose, the budding birch, and the hoary hawthorn, that I view and hang over with particular delight. I never hear the loud solitary 5 whistle of the curlew in a summer noon, or the wild mixing cadence of a troop of gray plover in an autumnal morning, without feeling an elevation of soul like the enthusiasm of devotion or poetry. Tell me, my dear friend, to what can this be owing? Are we a piece of machinery, which, like the 10 Æolian harp, passive, takes the impression of the passing accident; or do these workings argue something within us above the trodden clod? I own myself partial to such proofs of those awful and important realities: a God that made all things, man's immaterial and immortal nature, and a world of 15 weal or wo beyond death and the grave.'

Force and fineness of understanding are often spoken of as something different from general force and fineness of nature, as something partly independent of them. The necessities of language so require it ; but in truth these 20 qualities are not distinct and independent; except in special cases, and from special causes, they ever go together. A man of strong understanding is generally a man of strong character; neither is delicacy in the one kind often divided from delicacy in the other. No one, 25 at all events, is ignorant that in the Poetry of Burns keenness of insight keeps pace with keenness of feeling; that his *light* is not more pervading than his *warmth*. He is a man of the most impassioned temper ; with passions not strong only, but noble, and of the sort in 30 which great virtues and great poems take their rise. It is reverence, it is love towards all Nature that inspires him, that opens his eyes to its beauty, and makes heart and voice eloquent in its praise. There is a true old

saying, that 'Love furthers knowledge:' but, above all, it
is the living essence of that knowledge which makes
poets; the first principle of its existence, increase, activity. Of Burns's fervid affection, his generous all-em-
5 bracing Love, we have spoken already, as of the grand
distinction of his nature, seen equally in word and deed,
in his Life and in his Writings.   It were easy to multiply
examples.   Not man only, but all that environs man in
the material and moral universe, is lovely in his sight :
10 'the hoary hawthorn,' the 'troop of gray plover,' the
'solitary curlew,' all are dear to him; all live in this
Earth along with him, and to all he is knit as in mysterious brotherhood.   How touching is it, for instance, that,
amidst the gloom of personal misery, brooding over the
15 wintry desolation without him and within him, he thinks
of the 'ourie [1] cattle' and 'silly sheep,' and their sufferings in the pitiless storm !

> I thought me on the ourie cattle,
> Or silly sheep, wha bide this brattle
> 20   O' wintry war,
> Or thro' the drift, deep-lairing, [2] sprattle, [3]
>   Beneath a scaur. [4]
> Ilk [5] happing bird, wee helpless thing,
> That in the merry months o' spring
> 25   Delighted me to hear thee sing,
>   What comes o' thee ?
> Where wilt thou cow'r thy chittering [6] wing,
>   And close thy ee?

The tenant of the mean hut, with its 'ragged roof and
30 chinky wall,' has a heart to pity even these !   This is

---

[1] Shivering.   [4] Cliff.
[2] Wading.   [5] Each.
[3] Struggle.   Trembling with cold.

worth several homilies on Mercy; for it is the voice of
Mercy herself. Burns, indeed, lives in sympathy; his
soul rushes forth into all realms of being; nothing that
has existence can be indifferent to him. The very Devil
he cannot hate with right orthodoxy:

> But fare you weel, auld Nickie-ben;
> O, wad ye tak a thought and men'!
> Ye aiblins[1] might,— I dinna ken,—
>   Still hae a stake;
> I'm wae to think upo' yon den,
>   Even for your sake!

"*He* is the father of curses and lies," said Dr. Slop;
"and is cursed and damned already." "I am sorry for
it," quoth my uncle Toby!— a Poet without Love were
a physical and metaphysical impossibility.

But has it not been said, in contradiction to this principle, that 'Indignation makes verses'? It has been so
said, and is true enough: but the contradiction is
apparent, not real. The Indignation which makes
verses is, properly speaking, an inverted Love; the love
of some right, some worth, some goodness, belonging to
ourselves or others, which has been injured, and which
this tempestuous feeling issues forth to defend and
avenge. No selfish fury of heart, existing there as a
primary feeling, and without its opposite, ever produced
much Poetry: otherwise, we suppose, the Tiger were the
most musical of all our choristers. Johnson said, he
loved a good hater; by which he must have meant, not
so much one that hated violently, as one that hated
wisely; hated baseness from love of nobleness. However, in spite of Johnson's paradox, tolerable enough for
once in speech, but which need not have been so often

---

[1] Perhaps.

adopted in print since then, we rather believe that good
men deal sparingly in hatred, either wise or unwise : nay
that a 'good hater' is still a desideratum in this world.
The Devil, at least, who passes for the chief and best of
that class, is said to be nowise an amiable character.

Of the verses which Indignation makes, Burns has also
given us specimens : and among the best that were ever
given. Who will forget his '*Dweller in yon Dungeon
dark;*' a piece that might have been chanted by the
Furies of Æschylus ?   The secrets of the infernal Pit are
laid bare ; a boundless baleful 'darkness visible ;' and
streaks of hell-fire quivering madly in its black haggard
bosom !

> Dweller in yon Dungeon dark,
> Hangman of Creation, mark !
> Who in widow's weeds appears,
> Laden with unhonoured years,
> Noosing with care a bursting purse,
> Baited with many a deadly curse !

Why should we speak of *Scots wha hae wi' Wallace bled;*
since all know of it, from the king to the meanest of his
subjects ? This dithyrambic was composed on horse-
back ; in riding in the middle of tempests, over the
wildest Galloway moor, in company with a Mr. Syme,
who, observing the poet's looks, forbore to speak,—
judiciously enough, for a man composing *Bruce's Address*
might be unsafe to trifle with.   Doubtless this stern
hymn was singing itself, as he formed it, through the
soul of Burns : but to the external ear, it should be sung
with the throat of the whirlwind.   So long as there is
warm blood in the heart of Scotchman or man, it will
move in fierce thrills under this war-ode ; the best, we
believe, that was ever written by any pen.

Another wild stormful Song, that dwells in our ear and
mind with a strange tenacity, is *Macpherson's Farewell.*
Perhaps there is something in the tradition itself that co-
operates. For was not this grim Celt, this shaggy North-
land Cacus, that 'lived a life of sturt and strife, and died   5
by treacherie,' — was not he too one of the Nimrods and
Napoleons of the earth, in the arena of his own remote
misty glens, for want of a clearer and wider one? Nay,
was there not a touch of grace given him? A fibre of
love and softness, of poetry itself, must have lived in his 10
savage heart: for he composed that air the night before
his execution; on the wings of that poor melody his better soul would soar away above oblivion, pain and all the
ignominy and despair, which, like an avalanche, was hurl-
ing him to the abyss! Here also, as at Thebes, and in   15
Pelops' line, was material Fate matched against man's
Free-will; matched in bitterest though obscure duel;
and the ethereal soul sank not, even in its blindness, without a cry which has survived it. But who, except Burns,
could have given words to such a soul; words that we   20
never listen to without a strange half-barbarous, half-
poetic fellow-feeling?

> Sae rantingly,[1] sae wantonly,
>   Sae dauntingly gaed he;
> He play'd a spring, and danced it round,   25
>   Below the gallows-tree.

Under a lighter disguise, the same principle of Love,
which we have recognised as the great characteristic of
Burns, and of all true poets, occasionally manifests itself
in the shape of Humour. Everywhere, indeed, in his   30
sunny moods, a full buoyant flood of mirth rolls through
the mind of Burns; he rises to the high, and stoops to

---

[1] Gleefully.

the low, and is brother and playmate to all Nature. We
speak not of his bold and often irresistible faculty of car-
icature; for this is Drollery rather than Humour: but a
much tenderer sportfulness dwells in him; and comes
5 forth here and there, in evanescent and beautiful touches;
as in his *Address to the Mouse,* or the *Farmer's Mare,* or
in his *Elegy on poor Mailie,* which last may be reckoned
his happiest effort of this kind. In these pieces there
are traits of a Humour as fine as that of Sterne; yet
10 altogether different, original, peculiar, — the Humour of
Burns.

Of the tenderness, the playful pathos, and many other
kindred qualities of Burns's Poetry, much more might be
said; but now, with these poor outlines of a sketch, we
15 must prepare to quit this part of our subject. To speak
of his individual Writings, adequately and with any detail, would lead us far beyond our limits. As already
hinted, we can look on but few of these pieces as, in
strict critical language, deserving the name of Poems:

20 they are rhymed eloquence, rhymed pathos, rhymed sense;
yet seldom essentially melodious, aerial, poetical. *Tam
o' Shanter* itself, which enjoys so high a favour, does not
appear to us at all decisively to come under this last cat-
egory. It is not so much a poem, as a piece of spark-
25 ling rhetoric; the heart and body of the story still lies
hard and dead. He has not gone back, much less car-
ried us back, into that dark, earnest, wondering age, when
the tradition was believed, and when it took its rise; he
does not attempt, by any new-modeling of his supernat-
30 ural ware, to strike anew that deep mysterious chord of
human nature, which once responded to such things;
and which lives in us too, and will forever live, though
silent now, or vibrating with far other notes, and to far
different issues. Our German readers will understand us,

when we say, that he is not the Tieck but the Musäus of this tale. Externally it is all green and living; yet look closer, it is no firm growth, but only ivy on a rock. The piece does not properly cohere : the strange chasm which yawns in our incredulous imaginations between the Ayr public-house and the gate of Tophet, is nowhere bridged over, nay the idea of such a bridge is laughed at ; and thus the Tragedy of the adventure becomes a mere drunken phantasmagoria, or many-coloured spectrum painted on ale-vapours, and the Farce alone has any reality. We do not say that Burns should have made much more of this tradition ; we rather think that, for strictly poetical purposes, not much *was* to be made of it. Neither are we blind to the deep, varied, genial power displayed in what he has actually accomplished ; but we find far more 'Shakspearean' qualities, as these of *Tam o'Shanter* have been fondly named, in many of his other pieces ; nay we incline to believe that this latter might have been written, all but quite as well, by a man who, in place of genius, had only possessed talent.

Perhaps we may venture to say, that the most strictly poetical of all his 'poems' is one which does not appear in Currie's Edition ; but has been often printed before and since, under the humble title of *The Jolly Beggars*. The subject truly is among the lowest in Nature; but it only the more shows our Poet's gift in raising it into the domain of Art. To our minds, this piece seems thoroughly compacted ; melted together, refined; and poured forth in one flood of true *liquid* harmony. It is light, airy, soft of movement ; yet sharp and precise in its details ; every face is a portrait : that *raucle carlin*, that *wee Apollo*, that *Son of Mars*, are Scottish, yet ideal; the scene is at once a dream, and the very Ragcastle of 'Poosie-Nansie.' Farther, it seems in a considerable

degree complete, a real self-supporting Whole, which **is**
the highest merit in a poem.   The blanket of the Night
is drawn asunder for a moment; in full, ruddy, flaming
light, these rough tatterdemalions are seen in their boisterous revel; for the strong pulse of Life vindicates its
right to gladness even here ; and when the curtain closes,
we prolong the action, without effort ; the next day as
the last, our *Caird* and our *Balladmonger* are singing and
soldiering; their 'brats[1] and callets'[2] are hawking, begging, cheating ; and some other night, in new combinations,
they will wring from Fate another hour of wassail and
good cheer.   Apart from the universal sympathy with
man which this again bespeaks in Burns, a genuine in-
spiration and no inconsiderable technical talent are manifested here.   There is the fidelity, humour, warm life
and accurate painting and grouping of some Teniers, for
whom hostlers and carousing peasants are not without
significance.   It would be strange, doubtless, to call this
the best of Burns's writings : we mean to say only, that
it seems to us the most perfect of its kind, as a piece of
poetical composition, strictly so called.   In the *Beggars'*
Opera, in the *Beggars' Bush*, as other critics have already
remarked, there is nothing which, in real poetic vigour,
equals this *Cantata ;* nothing, as we think, which comes
within many degrees of it.

But by far the most finished, complete and truly inspired pieces of Burns are, without dispute, to be found
among his *Songs*.   It is here that, although through a
small aperture, his light shines with least obstruction ; in
its highest beauty and pure sunny clearness.   The reason
may be, that Song is a brief simple species of composition ; and requires nothing so much for its perfection as

[1] Rags.   [2] Wenches.

genuine poetic feeling, genuine music of heart. Yet the Song has its rules equally with the Tragedy; rules which in most cases are poorly fulfilled, in many cases are not so much as felt. We might write a long essay on the Songs of Burns; which we reckon by far the best that Britain has yet produced: for indeed, since the era of Queen Elizabeth, we know not that, by any other hand, aught truly worth attention has been accomplished in this department. True, we have songs enough 'by persons of quality'; we have tawdry, hollow, wine-bred madrigals; many a rhymed speech 'in the flowing and watery vein of Ossorius the Portugal Bishop,' rich in sonorous words, and, for moral, dashed perhaps with some tint of a sentimental sensuality; all which many persons cease not from endeavouring to sing; though for most part, we fear, the music is but from the throat outwards, or at best from some region far enough short of the *Soul;* not in which, but in a certain inane Limbo of the Fancy, or even in some vaporous debateable-land on the outskirts of the Nervous System, most of such madrigals and rhymed speeches seem to have originated.

With the Songs of Burns we must not name these things. Independently of the clear, manly, heartfelt sentiment that ever pervades *his* poetry, his Songs are honest in another point of view: in form, as well as in spirit. They do not *affect* to be set to music, but they actually and in themselves are music; they have received their life, and fashioned themselves together, in the medium of Harmony, as Venus rose from the bosom of the sea. The story, the feeling, is not detailed, but suggested; not *said*, or spouted, in rhetorical completeness and coherence; but *sung*, in fitful gushes, in glowing hints, in fantastic breaks, in *warblings* not of the voice only, but of the whole mind. We consider this to be the essence

of a song; and that no songs since the little careless
catches, and as it were drops of song, which Shakspeare
has here and there sprinkled over his Plays, fulfil this
condition in nearly the same degree as most of Burns's
5 do. Such grace and truth of external movement, too,
presupposes in general a corresponding force and truth
of sentiment and inward meaning. The Songs of Burns
are not more perfect in the former quality than in the
latter. With what tenderness he sings, yet with what
10 vehemence and entireness! There is a piercing wail in
his sorrow, the purest rapture in his joy; he burns with
the sternest ire, or laughs with the loudest or sliest
mirth; and yet he is sweet and soft, ' sweet as the smile
when fond lovers meet, and soft as their parting tear.'
15 If we farther take into account the immense variety of
his subjects; how, from the loud flowing revel in *Willie
brew'd a Peck o' Maut*, to the still, rapt enthusiasm of sadness for *Mary in Heaven;* from the glad kind greeting of
Auld Langsyne, or the comic archness of *Duncan Gray*,
20 to the fire-eyed fury of *Scots wha hae wi' Wallace bled*,
he has found a tone and words for every mood of man's
heart,— it will seem a small praise if we rank him as the
first of all our Song-writers; for we know not where to
find one worthy of being second to him.

25   It is on his songs, as we believe, that Burns's chief
influence as an author will ultimately be found to de-
pend : nor, if our Fletcher's aphorism is true, shall we
account this a small influence. ' Let me make the songs
of a people,' said he, ' and you shall make its laws.'
30 Surely, if ever any Poet might have equalled himself with
Legislators on this ground, it was Burns. His Songs are
already part of the mother-tongue, not of Scotland only
but of Britain, and of the millions that in all ends of the
earth speak a British language. In hut and hall, as the

heart unfolds itself in many-coloured joy and woe of existence, the *name*, the *voice* of that joy and that woe, is the name and voice which Burns has given them. Strictly speaking, perhaps no British man has so deeply affected the thoughts and feelings of so many men, as this solitary and altogether private individual, with means apparently the humblest.

In another point of view, moreover, we incline to think that Burns's influence may have been considerable : we mean, as exerted specially on the Literature of his coun- try, at least on the Literature of Scotland. Among the great changes which British, particularly Scottish litera- ture, has undergone since that period, one of the greatest will be found to consist in its remarkable increase of nationality. Even the English writers, most popular in Burns's time, were little distinguished for their literary patriotism, in this its best sense. A certain attenuated cosmopolitanism had, in good measure, taken place of the old insular home-feeling ; literature was, as it were, with- out any local environment ; was not nourished by the affections which spring from a native soil. Our Grays and Glovers seemed to write almost as if *in vacuo ;* the thing written bears no mark of place ; it is not written so much for Englishmen, as for men ; or rather, which is the inevitable result of this, for certain Generalisations which philosophy termed men. Goldsmith is an excep- tion : not so Johnson ; the scene of his *Rambler* is little more English than that of his *Rasselas.*

But if such was, in some degree, the case with England, it was, in the highest degree, the case with Scotland. In fact, our Scottish literature had, at that period, a very singular aspect ; unexampled, so far as we know, except perhaps at Geneva, where the same state of matters ap- pears still to continue. For a long period after Scotland

became British, we had no literature : at the date when
Addison and Steele were writing their *Spectators*, our good
John Boston was writing, with the noblest intent, but
alike in defiance of grammar and philosophy, his *Four-*
5 *fold State of Man.* Then came the schisms in our
National Church, and the fiercer schisms in our Body
Politic : Theologic ink, and Jacobite blood, with gall
enough in both cases, seemed to have blotted out the
intellect of the country : however, it was only obscured,
10 not obliterated. Lord Kames made nearly the first
attempt at writing English ; and ere long, Hume, Robertson, Smith, and a whole host of followers, attracted hither
the eyes of all Europe. And yet in this brilliant resus-
citation of our 'fervid genius,' there was nothing truly
15 Scottish, nothing indigenous ; except, perhaps, the natural
impetuosity of intellect, which we sometimes claim, and
are sometimes upbraided with, as a characteristic of our
nation. It is curious to remark that Scotland, so full of
writers, had no Scottish culture, nor indeed any English ;
20 our culture was almost exclusively French. It was by
studying Racine and Voltaire, Batteux and Boileau, that
Kames had trained himself to be a critic and philosopher ;
it was the light of Montesquieu and Mably that guided
Robertson in his political speculations ; Quesnay's lamp
25 that kindled the lamp of Adam Smith. Hume was too
rich a man to borrow ; and perhaps he reacted on the
French more than he was acted on by them : but neither
had he aught to do with Scotland ; Edinburgh, equally
with La Flèche, was but the lodging and laboratory, in
30 which he not so much morally *lived*, as metaphysically
investigated. Never, perhaps, was there a class of writers
so clear and well-ordered, yet so totally destitute, to all
appearance, of any patriotic affection, nay of any human
affection whatever. The French wits of the period were

as unpatriotic : but their general deficiency in moral principle, not to say their avowed sensuality and unbelief in
all virtue, strictly so called, render this accountable
enough. We hope, there is a patriotism founded on
something better than prejudice ; that our country may 5
be dear to us, without injury to our philosophy ; that in
loving and justly prizing all other lands, we may prize
justly, and yet love before all others, our own stern
Motherland, and the venerable Structure of social and
moral Life, which Mind has through long ages been 10
building up for us there. Surely there is nourishment for
the better part of man's heart in all this : surely the roots,
that have fixed themselves in the very core of man's
being, may be so cultivated as to grow up not into briers,
but into roses, in the field of his life ! Our Scottish sages 15
have no such propensities : the field of their life shows
neither briers nor roses ; but only a flat, continuous
thrashing-floor for Logic, whereon all questions, from the
' Doctrine of Rent ' to the ' Natural History of Religion,'
are thrashed and sifted with the same mechanical im- 20
partiality !

With Sir Walter Scott at the head of our literature, it
cannot be denied that much of this evil is past, or rapidly
passing away : our chief literary men, whatever other
faults they may have, no longer live among us like a 25
French Colony, or some knot of Propaganda Missionaries ; but like natural-born subjects of the soil, partak-
ing and sympathising in all our attachments, humours
and habits. Our literature no longer grows in water but
in mould, and with the true racy virtues of the soil and 30
climate. How much of this change may be due to Burns,
or to any other individual, it might be difficult to estimate.
Direct literary imitation of Burns was not to be looked
for. But his example, in the fearless adoption of domes-

tic subjects, could not but operate from afar; and certainly in no heart did the love of country ever burn with
a warmer glow than in that of Burns: 'a tide of Scottish
prejudice,' as he modestly calls this deep and generous
5 feeling, 'had been poured along his veins; and he felt
that it would boil there till the flood-gates shut in eternal rest.' It seemed to him, as if *he* could do so little
for his country, and yet would so gladly have done all.
One small province stood open for him, — that of Scot-
10 tish Song; and how eagerly he entered on it, how de-
votedly he laboured there! In his toilsome journeyings,
this object never quits him; it is the little happy-valley
of his careworn heart. In the gloom of his own affliction, he eagerly searches after some lonely brother of the
15 muse, and rejoices to snatch one other name from the
oblivion that was covering it! These were early feelings,
and they abode with him to the end:

> . . . A wish (I mind its power),
> A wish, that to my latest hour
20 > Will strongly heave my breast, —
> That I, for poor auld Scotland's sake,
> Some useful plan or book could make,
> Or sing a sang at least.

> The rough bur Thistle spreading wide
25 >   Amang the bearded bear,
> I turn'd my weeding-clips aside,
>   And spared the symbol dear.

But to leave the mere literary character of Burns,
which has already detained us too long. Far more inter-
30 esting than any of his written works, as it appears to us,
are his acted ones: the Life he willed and was fated to
lead among his fellow-men. These Poems are but like
little rhymed fragments scattered here and there in the

grand unrhymed Romance of his earthly existence; and it is only when intercalated in this at their proper places, that they attain their full measure of significance. And this, too, alas, was but a fragment! The plan of a mighty edifice had been sketched; some columns, porticos, firm masses of building, stand completed; the rest more or less clearly indicated; with many a far-stretching tendency, which only studious and friendly eyes can now trace towards the purposed termination. For the work is broken off in the middle, almost in the beginning; and rises among us, beautiful and sad, at once unfinished and a ruin! If charitable judgment was necessary in estimating his Poems, and justice required that the aim and the manifest power to fulfil it must often be accepted for the fulfilment; much more is this the case in regard to his Life, the sum and result of all his endeavours, where his difficulties came upon him not in detail only, but in mass; and so much has been left unaccomplished, nay was mistaken, and altogether marred.

Properly speaking, there is but one era in the life of Burns, and that the earliest. We have not youth and manhood, but only youth: for, to the end, we discern no decisive change in the complexion of his character; in his thirty-seventh year, he is still, as it were, in youth. With all that resoluteness of judgment, that penetrating insight, and singular maturity of intellectual power, exhibited in his writings, he never attains to any clearness regarding himself; to the last, he never ascertains his peculiar aim, even with such distinctness as is common among ordinary men; and therefore never can pursue it with that singleness of will, which insures success and some contentment to such men. To the last, he wavers between two purposes: glorying in his talent, like a true poet, he yet cannot consent to make this his chief and

sole glory, and to follow it as the one thing needful, through poverty or riches, through good or evil report. Another far meaner ambition still cleaves to him ; he must dream and struggle about a certain 'Rock of Inde-
5 pendence ; ' which, natural and even admirable as it might be, was still but a warring with the world, on the comparatively insignificant ground of his being more completely or less completely supplied with money than others ; of his standing at a higher or at a lower altitude
10 in general estimation than others. For the world still appears to him, as to the young, in borrowed colours: he expects from it what it cannot give to any man ; seeks for contentment, not within himself, in action and wise effort, but from without, in the kindness of circumstances,
15 in love, friendship, honour, pecuniary ease. He would be happy, not actively and in himself, but passively and from some ideal cornucopia of Enjoyments, not earned by his own labour, but showered on him by the beneficence of Destiny. Thus, like a young man, he cannot gird
20 himself up for any worthy well-calculated goal, but swerves to and fro, between passionate hope and re-morseful disappointment : rushing onwards with a deep tempestuous force, he surmounts or breaks asunder many a barrier ; travels, nay advances far, but advancing only
25 under uncertain guidance, is ever and anon turned from his path ; and to the last cannot reach the only true hap-piness of a man, that of clear decided Activity in the sphere for which, by nature and circumstances, he has been fitted and appointed.

30 We do not say these things in dispraise of Burns ; nay, perhaps, they but interest us the more in his favour. This blessing is not given soonest to the best ; but rather, it is often the greatest minds that are latest in obtaining it ; for where most is to be developed, most time may be

required to develop it. A complex condition had been assigned him from without ; as complex a condition from within : no 'preëstablished harmony' existed between the clay soil of Mossgiel and the empyrean soul of Robert Burns ; it was not wonderful that the adjustment between them should have been long postponed, and his arm long cumbered, and his sight confused, in so vast and discordant an economy as he had been appointed steward over. Byron was, at his death, but a year younger than Burns ; and through life, as it might have appeared, far more simply situated : yet in him too we can trace no such adjustment, no such moral manhood; but at best, and only a little before his end, the beginning of what seemed such.

By much the most striking incident in Burns's Life is his journey to Edinburgh; but perhaps a still more important one is his residence at Irvine, so early as in his twenty-third year. Hitherto his life had been poor and toilworn ; but otherwise not ungenial, and, with all its distresses, by no means unhappy. In his parentage, deducting outward circumstances, he had every reason to reckon himself fortunate. (His father was a man of thoughtful, intense, earnest character, as the best of our peasants are ; valuing knowledge, possessing some, and what is far better and rarer, openminded for more : a man with a keen insight and devout heart ; reverent towards God, friendly therefore at once, and fearless towards all that God has made : in one word, though but a hard-handed peasant, a complete and fully unfolded *Man.*) Such a father is seldom found in any rank in society ; and was worth descending far in society to seek. Unfortunately, he was very poor ; had he been even a little richer, almost never so little, the whole might have issued far otherwise. Mighty events

turn on a straw; the crossing of a brook decides the con-
quest of the world. Had this William Burns's small
seven acres of nursery-ground anywise prospered, the boy
Robert had been sent to school; had struggled forward,
as so many weaker men do, to some university; come
forth not as a rustic wonder, but as a regular well-trained
intellectual workman, and changed the whole course of
British Literature, — for it lay in him to have done this !
But the nursery did not prosper; poverty sank his
whole family below the help of even our cheap school-
system : Burns remained a hard-worked ploughboy, and
British literature took its own course. Nevertheless,
even in this rugged scene there is much to nourish him.
If he drudges, it is with his brother, and for his father
and mother, whom he loves, and would fain shield from
want. Wisdom is not banished from their poor hearth,
nor the balm of natural feeling: the solemn words, *Let
us worship God*, are heard there from a 'priest-like
father'; if threatenings or unjust men throw mother and
children into tears, these are tears not of grief only, but
of holiest affection ; every heart in that humble group
feels itself the closer knit to every other ; in their hard
warfare they are there together, a 'little band of breth-
ren.' Neither are such tears, and the deep beauty that
dwells in them, their only portion. Light visits the
hearts as it does the eyes of all living: there is a force,
too, in this youth, that enables him to trample on misfortune; nay to bind it under his feet to make him sport.
For a bold, warm, buoyant humour of character has been
given him ; and so the thick-coming shapes of evil are
welcomed with a gay, friendly irony, and in their closest
pressure he bates no jot of heart or hope. Vague yearn-
ings of ambition fail not, as he grows up ; dreamy fancies
hang like cloud-cities around him; the curtain of Exist-

ence is slowly rising, in many-coloured splendour and
gloom : and the auroral light of first love is gilding his
horizon, and the music of song is on his path ; and so he
walks

> . . . . . . in glory and in joy,
> Behind his plough, upon the mountain side.

5

We ourselves know, from the best evidence, that up to
this date Burns was happy; nay that he was the gayest,
brightest, most fantastic, fascinating being to be found
in the world ; more so even than he ever afterwards 10
appeared.   But now, at this early age, he quits the pa-
ternal roof ; goes forth into looser, louder, more exciting
society ; and becomes initiated in those dissipations,
those vices, which a certain class of philosophers have
asserted to be a natural preparative for entering on active 15
life ; a kind of mud-bath, in which the youth is, as it
were, necessitated to steep, and, we suppose, cleanse
himself, before the real toga of Manhood can be laid on
him.   We shall not dispute much with this class of philosophers ; we hope they are mistaken ; for Sin and Re- 20
morse so easily beset us at all stages of life, and are
always such indifferent company, that it seems hard we
should, at any stage, be forced and fated not only to
meet but to yield to them, and even serve for a term in
their leprous armada.   We hope it is not so.   Clear we 25
are, at all events, it cannot be the training one receives
in this Devil's service, but only our determining to desert
from it, that fits us for true manly Action.   We become
men, not after we have been dissipated, and disappointed
in the chase of false pleasure ; but after we have ascer- 30
tained, in any way, what impassable barriers hem us in
through this life ; how mad it is to hope for contentment to our infinite soul from the *gifts* of this extremely

finite world; that a man must be sufficient for himself;
and that for suffering and enduring there is no remedy
but striving and doing.   Manhood begins when we have
in any way made truce with Necessity; begins even
5 when we have surrendered to Necessity, as the most part
only do; but begins joyfully and hopefully only when
we have reconciled ourselves to Necessity; and thus, in
reality, triumphed over it, and felt that in Necessity we
are free.   Surely, such lessons as this last, which, in one
10 shape or other, is the grand lesson for every mortal man,
are better learned from the lips of a devout mother, in
the looks and actions of a devout father, while the heart
is yet soft and pliant, than in collision with the sharp
adamant of Fate, attracting us to shipwreck us, when the
15 heart is grown hard, and may be broken before it will
become contrite.   Had Burns continued to learn this, as
he was already learning it, in his father's cottage, he
would have learned it fully, which he never did; and
been saved many a lasting aberration, many a bitter hour
20 and year of remorseful sorrow.

It seems to us another circumstance of fatal import in
Burns's history, that at this time too he became involved
in the religious quarrels of his district; that he was
enlisted and feasted, as the fighting man of the New-
25 Light Priesthood, in their highly unprofitable warfare.
At the tables of these free-minded clergy he learned much
more than was needful for him.   Such liberal ridicule of
fanaticism awakened in his mind scruples about Religion
itself; and a whole world of Doubts, which it required
30 quite another set of conjurors than these men to exor-
cise.   We do not say that such an intellect as his could
have escaped similar doubts at some period of his
history; or even that he could, at a later period, have
come through them altogether victorious and unharmed:

but it seems peculiarly unfortunate that this time, above all others, should have been fixed for the encounter. For now, with principles assailed by evil example from without, by 'passions raging like demons' from within, he had little need of sceptical misgivings to whisper treason in the heat of the battle, or to cut off his retreat if he were already defeated. He loses his feeling of innocence ; his mind is at variance with itself ; the old divinity no longer presides there ; but wild Desires and wild Repentance alternately oppress him. Ere long, too, he has committed himself before the world ; his character for sobriety, dear to a Scottish peasant as few corrupted worldlings can even conceive, is destroyed in the eyes of men ; and his only refuge consists in trying to disbelieve his guiltiness, and is but a refuge of lies. The blackest desperation now gathers over him, broken only by red lightnings of remorse. The whole fabric of his life is blasted asunder ; for now not only his character, but his personal liberty, is to be lost ; men and Fortune are leagued for his hurt ; 'hungry Ruin has him in the wind.' He sees no escape but the saddest of all : exile from his loved country, to a country in every sense inhospitable and abhorrent to him. While the ' gloomy night is gathering fast,' in mental storm and solitude, as well as in physical, he sings his wild farewell to Scotland :

> Farewell, my friends ; farewell, my foes !
> My peace with these, my love with those :
> The bursting tears my heart declare ;
> Adieu, my native banks of Ayr !

Light breaks suddenly in on him in floods ; but still a false transitory light, and no real sunshine. He is invited to Edinburgh ; hastens thither with anticipating heart ; is welcomed as in a triumph, and with universal

blandishment and acclamation ; whatever is wisest, whatever is greatest or loveliest there, gathers round him, to
gaze on his face, to show him honour, sympathy, affection.
Burns's appearance among the sages and nobles of
5 Edinburgh must be regarded as one of the most singular
phenomena in modern Literature ; almost like the
appearance of some Napoleon among the crowned sovereigns of modern Politics. For it is nowise as ' a mockery
king,' set there by favour, transiently and for a pur-
10 pose, that he will let himself be treated ; still less is
he a mad Rienzi, whose sudden elevation turns his too
weak head : but he stands there on his own basis ; cool,
unastonished, holding his equal rank from Nature herself ;
putting forth no claim which there is not strength *in* him,
15 as well as about him, to vindicate. Mr. Lockhart has
some forcible observations on this point :

' It needs no effort of imagination,' says he, ' to conceive
what the sensations of an isolated set of scholars (almost all
either clergymen or professors) must have been in the presence
20 of this big-boned, black-browed, brawny stranger, with his
great flashing eyes, who, having forced his way among them
from the plough-tail at a single stride, manifested in the whole
strain of his bearing and conversation a most thorough con-
viction, that in the society of the most eminent men of his
25 nation he was exactly where he was entitled to be ; hardly
deigned to flatter them by exhibiting even an occasional symp-
tom of being flattered by their notice ; by turns calmly
measured himself against the most cultivated understandings
of his time in discussion ; overpowered the *bon mots* of the
30 most celebrated convivialists by broad floods of merriment,
impregnated with all the burning life of genius ; astounded
bosoms habitually enveloped in the thrice-piled folds of social
reserve, by compelling them to tremble,— nay, to tremble
visibly,— beneath the fearless touch of natural pathos ; and
35 all this without indicating the smallest willingness to be ranked

among those professional ministers of excitement, who are content to be paid in money and smiles for doing what the spectators and auditors would be ashamed of doing in their own persons, even if they had the power of doing it ; and last, and probably worst of all, who was known to be in the habit of enlivening societies which they would have scorned to approach, still more frequently than their own, with eloquence no less magnificent ; with wit, in all likelihood still more daring ; often enough, as the superiors whom he fronted without alarm might have guessed from the beginning, and had ere long no occasion to guess, with wit pointed at themselves.'

The farther we remove from this scene, the more singular will it seem to us : details of the exterior aspect of it are already full of interest. Most readers recollect Mr. Walker's personal interviews with Burns as among the best passages of his Narrative : a time will come when this reminiscence of Sir Walter Scott's, slight though it is, will also be precious :

'As for Burns,' writes Sir Walter, 'I may truly say, *Virgilium vidi tantùm.* I was a lad of fifteen in 1786–7, when he came first to Edinburgh, but had sense and feeling enough to be much interested in his poetry, and would have given the world to know him : but I had very little acquaintance with any literary people, and still less with the gentry of the west country, the two sets that he most frequented. Mr. Thomas Grierson was at that time a clerk of my father's. He knew Burns, and promised to ask him to his lodgings to dinner ; but had no opportunity to keep his word ; otherwise I might have seen more of this distinguished man. As it was, I saw him one day at the late venerable Professor Ferguson's, where there were several gentlemen of literary reputation, among whom I remember the celebrated Mr. Dugald Stewart. Of course, we youngsters sat silent, looked and listened. The only thing I remember which was remarkable in Burns's manner, was the effect produced upon him by a print of

Bunbury's, representing a soldier lying dead on the snow, his
dog sitting in misery on one side,— on the other, his widow,
with a child in her arms.   These lines were written beneath :

> " Cold on Canadian hills, or Minden's plain,
> 5   Perhaps that mother wept her soldier slain ;
>   Bent o'er her babe, her eye dissolved in dew,
>   The big drops mingling with the milk he drew,
>   Gave the sad pressage of his future years,
>   The child of misery baptised in tears."

10   ' Burns seemed much affected by the print, or rather by the
ideas which it suggested to his mind.   He actually shed tears.
He asked whose the lines were ; and it chanced that nobody
but myself remembered that they occur in a half-forgotten
poem of Langhorne's called by the unpromising title of " The
15 Justice of Peace."   I whispered my information to a friend
present ; he mentioned it to Burns, who rewarded me with
a look and a word, which, though of mere civility, I then received and still recollect with very great pleasure.

   ' His person was strong and robust ; his manners rustic,
20 not clownish ; a sort of dignified plainness and simplicity,
which received part of its effect perhaps from one's knowledge
of his extraordinary talents.   His features are represented in
Mr. Nasmyth's picture : but to me it conveys the idea that
they are diminished, as if seen in perspective.   I think his
25 countenance was more massive than it looks in any of the
portraits.   I should have taken the poet, had I not known what
he was, for a very sagacious country farmer of the old Scotch
school, *i.e.* none of your modern agriculturists who keep
labourers for their drudgery, but the *douce* [1] *gudeman* who held
30 his own plough.   There was a strong expression of sense and
shrewdness in all his lineaments ; the eye alone, I think, indicated the poetical character and temperament.   It was
large, and of a dark cast, which glowed (I say literally *glowed*)
when he spoke with feeling or interest.   I never saw such
35 another eye in a human head, though I have seen the most

· [1] Sedate.

distinguished men of my time. His conversation expressed perfect self-confidence, without the slightest presumption. Among the men who were the most learned of their time and country, he expressed himself with perfect firmness, but without the least intrusive forwardness; and when he differed in opinion, he did not hesitate to express it firmly, yet at the same time with modesty. I do not remember any part of his conversation distinctly enough to be quoted; nor did I ever see him again, except in the street, where he did not recognise me, as I could not expect he should. He was much caressed in Edinburgh: but (considering what literary emoluments have been since his day) the efforts made for his relief were extremely trifling.

' I remember, on this occasion I mention, I thought Burns's acquaintance with English poetry was rather limited; and also that, having twenty times the abilities of Allan Ramsay and of Ferguson, he talked of them with too much humility as his models: there was doubtless national predilection in his estimate.

' This is all I can tell you about Burns. I have only to add, that his dress corresponded with his manner. He was like a farmer dressed in his best to dine with the laird. I do not speak *in malam partem*, when I say, I never saw a man in company with his superiors in station or information more perfectly free from either the reality or the affectation of embarrassment. I was told, but did not observe it, that his address to females was extremely deferential, and always with a turn either to the pathetic or humorous, which engaged their attention particularly. I have heard the late Duchess of Gordon remark this. I do not know anything I can add to these recollections of forty years since.'

The conduct of Burns under this dazzling blaze of favour; the calm, unaffected, manly manner in which he not only bore it, but estimated its value, has justly been regarded as the best proof that could be given of his real vigour and integrity of mind. A little natural vanity,

some touches of hypocritical modesty, some glimmerings
of affectation, at least some fear of being thought affected,
we could have pardoned in almost any man ; but no such
indication is to be traced here.   In his unexampled situ-
5 ation the young peasant is not a moment perplexed ; so
many strange lights do not confuse him, do not lead him
astray.   Nevertheless, we cannot but perceive that this
winter did him great and lasting injury.   A somewhat
clearer knowledge of men's affairs, scarcely of their char-
10 acters, it did afford him ; but a sharper feeling of
Fortune's unequal arrangements in their social destiny it
also left with him.   He had seen the gay and gorgeous
arena, in which the powerful are born to play their parts ;
nay had himself stood in the midst of it ; and he felt more
15 bitterly than ever, that here he was but a looker-on, and
had no part or lot in that splendid game.   From this time a
jealous indignant fear of social degradation takes posses-
sion of him ; and perverts, so far as aught could pervert,
his private contentment, and his feelings towards his
20 richer fellows.   It was clear to Burns that he had talent
enough to make a fortune, or a hundred fortunes, could
he but have rightly willed this ; it was clear also that he
willed something far different, and therefore could not
make one.   Unhappy it was that he had not power to
25 choose the one, and reject the other ; but must halt forever between two opinions, two objects ; making hampered advancement towards either.   But so is it with
many men : we 'long for the merchandise, yet would fain
keep the price ;' and so stand chaffering with Fate, in
30 vexatious altercation, till the night come, and our fair is
over !

The Edinburgh Learned of that period were in general
more noted for clearness of head than for warmth of
heart : with the exception of the good old Blacklock,

whose help was too ineffectual, scarcely one among them seems to have looked at Burns with any true sympathy, or indeed much otherwise than as at a highly curious *thing*. By the great also he is treated in the customary fashion ; entertained at their tables and dismissed : certain modica of pudding and praise are, from time to time, gladly exchanged for the fascination of his presence ; which exchange once effected, the bargain is finished, and each party goes his several way. At the end of this strange season, Burns gloomily sums up his gains and losses, and meditates on the chaotic future. In money he is somewhat richer ; in fame and the show of happiness, infinitely richer ; but in the substance of it, as poor as ever. Nay poorer ; for his heart is now maddened still more with the fever of worldly Ambition ; and through long years the disease will rack him with unprofitable sufferings, and weaken his strength for all true and nobler aims.

What Burns was next to do or to avoid ; how a man so circumstanced was now to guide himself towards his true advantage, might at this point of time have been a question for the wisest. It was a question too, which apparently he was left altogether to answer for himself : of his learned or rich patrons it had not struck any individual to turn a thought on this so trivial matter. Without claiming for Burns the praise of perfect sagacity, we must say, that his Excise and Farm scheme does not seem to us a very unreasonable one ; that we should be at a loss, even now, to suggest one decidedly better. Certain of his admirers have felt scandalised at his ever resolving to *gauge ;* and would have had him lie at the pool, till the spirit of Patronage stirred the waters, that so, with one friendly plunge, all his sorrows might be healed. Unwise counsellors ! They know not the manner of this

spirit; and how, in the lap of most golden dreams, a man
might have happiness, were it not that in the interim he
must die of hunger! It reflects credit on the manliness
and sound sense of Burns, that he felt so early on what
5 ground he was standing; and preferred self-help, on the
humblest scale, to dependence and inaction, though with
hope of far more splendid possibilities. But even these
possibilities were not rejected in his scheme : he might
expect, if it chanced that he *had* any friend, to rise, in no
10 long period, into something even like opulence and
leisure; while again, if it chanced that he had no friend, he
could still live in security; and for the rest, he 'did not
intend to borrow honour from any profession.' We reckon
that his plan was honest and well calculated: all turned on
15 the execution of it. Doubtless it failed; yet not, we believe, from any vice inherent in itself. Nay, after all, it
was no failure of external means, but of internal, that
overtook Burns. His was no bankruptcy of the purse, but
of the soul; to his last day, he owed no man anything.

20   Meanwhile he begins well : with two good and wise
actions. His donation to his mother, munificent from a
man whose income had lately been seven pounds a year,
was worthy of him, and not more than worthy. Generous
also, and worthy of him, was the treatment of the woman
25 whose life's welfare now depended on his pleasure. A
friendly observer might have hoped serene days for him :
his mind is on the true road to peace with itself : what
clearness he still wants will be given as he proceeds ;
for the best teacher of duties, that still lie dim to us, is
30 the Practice of those we see and have at hand. Had the
'patrons of genius,' who could give him nothing, but
taken nothing from him, at least nothing more! The
wounds of his heart would have healed, vulgar ambition
would have died away. Toil and Frugality would have

been welcome, since Virtue dwelt with them; and Poetry would have shone through them as of old : and in her clear ethereal light, which was his own by birthright, he might have looked down on his earthly destiny, and all its obstructions, not with patience only, but with love. 5

But the patrons of genius would not have it so. Picturesque tourists,[1] all manner of fashionable danglers after literature, and, far worse, all manner of convivial Mæcenases, hovered round him in his retreat; and his good as well as his weak qualities secured them influence 10 over him. He was flattered by their notice ; and his warm social nature made it impossible for him to shake them off, and hold on his way apart from them. These men, as we believe, were proximately the means of his ruin. Not that they meant him any ill ; they only meant 15 themselves a little good; if he suffered harm, let *him* look to it ! But they wasted his precious time and his precious talent; they disturbed his composure, broke down his returning habits of temperance and assiduous contented exertion. Their pampering was baneful to him; their 20

---

[1] There is one little sketch by certain 'English gentlemen' of this class, which, though adopted in Currie's Narrative, and since then repeated in most others, we have all along felt an invincible disposition to regard as imaginary : 'On a rock that projected into the stream, they saw a man employed in angling, of a singular appearance. He had a cap made of fox-skin on his head, a loose greatcoat fixed round him by a belt, from which depended an enormous Highland broad-sword. It was Burns.' Now, we rather think, it was *not* Burns. For, to say nothing of the fox-skin cap, the loose and quite Hibernian watchcoat with the belt, what are we to make of this 'enormous Highland broad-sword' depending from him ? More especially, as there is no word of parish constables on the outlook to see whether, as Dennis phrases it, he had an eye to his own midriff or that of the public ! Burns, of all men, had the least need, and the least tendency, to seek for distinction, either in his own eyes, or those of others, by such poor mummeries.

cruelty, which soon followed, was equally baneful. The old grudge against Fortune's inequality awoke with new bitterness in their neighbourhood; and Burns had no retreat but to 'the Rock of Independence,' which is but an

5 air-castle after all, that looks well at a distance, but will screen no one from real wind and wet. Flushed with irregular excitement, exasperated alternately by contempt of others, and contempt of himself, Burns was no longer regaining his peace of mind, but fast losing it forever.

10 There was a hollowness at the heart of his life, for his conscience did not now approve what he was doing.

Amid the vapours of unwise enjoyment, of bootless remorse, and angry discontent with Fate, his true loadstar, a life of Poetry, with Poverty, nay with Famine if it

15 must be so, was too often altogether hidden from his eyes. And yet he sailed a sea, where without some such loadstar there was no right steering. Meteors of French Politics rise before him, but these were not *his* stars. An accident this, which hastened, but did not originate, his

20 worst distresses. In the mad contentions of that time, he comes in collision with certain official Superiors; is wounded by them; cruelly lacerated, we should say, could a dead mechanical implement, in any case, be called cruel: and shrinks, in indignant pain, into deeper

25 self-seclusion, into gloomier moodiness than ever. His life has now lost its unity: it is a life of fragments; led with little aim, beyond the melancholy one of securing its own continuance, — in fits of wild false joy when such offered, and of black despondency when they passed

30 away. His character before the world begins to suffer: calumny is busy with him; for a miserable man makes more enemies than friends. Some faults he has fallen into, and a thousand misfortunes; but deep criminality is what he stands accused of, and they that are *not* with-

out sin cast the first stone at him ! For is he not a well-wisher to the French Revolution, a Jacobin, and therefore in that one act guilty of all? These accusations, political and moral, it has since appeared, were false enough : but the world hesitated little to credit them. Nay his convivial Mæcenases themselves were not the last to do it. There is reason to believe that, in his later years, the Dumfries Aristocracy had partly withdrawn themselves from Burns, as from a tainted person, no longer worthy of their acquaintance. That painful class, stationed, in all provincial cities, behind the outmost breastwork of Gentility, there to stand siege and do battle against the intrusions of Grocerdom and Grazierdom, had actually seen dishonour in the society of Burns, and branded him with their veto ; had, as we vulgarly say, *cut* him ! We find one passage in this Work of Mr. Lockhart's, which will not out of our thoughts :

'A gentleman of that county, whose name I have already more than once had occasion to refer to, has often told me that he was seldom more grieved, than when riding into Dumfries one fine summer evening about this time to attend a county ball, he saw Burns walking alone, on the shady side of the principal street of the town, while the opposite side was gay with successive groups of gentlemen and ladies, all drawn together for the festivities of the night, not one of whom appeared willing to recognise him. The horseman dismounted, and joined Burns, who on his proposing to cross the street said : " Nay, nay, my young friend, that's all over now; " and quoted, after a pause, some verses of Lady Grizzel Baillie's pathetic ballad :

> " His bonnet stood ance fu' fair on his brow,
> His auld ane look'd better than mony ane's new;
> But now he lets 't wear ony way it will hing,
> And casts himsell dowie [1] upon the corn-bing.

[1] Worn-out.

> O, were we young as we ance hae been,
> We sud hae been galloping down on yon green,
> And linking[1] it ower the lily-white lea !
> *And werena my heart light, I wad die.*"

It was little in Burns's character to let his feelings on certain
subjects escape in this fashion.   He, immediately after recit-
ing these verses, assumed the sprightliness of his most pleasing
manner; and taking his young friend home with him, entertained him very agreeably till the hour of the ball arrived.'

Alas ! when we think that Burns now sleeps 'where
bitter indignation can no longer lacerate his heart,'[2] and
that most of those fair dames and frizzled gentlemen
already lie at his side, where the breastwork of gentility
is quite thrown down, — who would not sigh over the
thin delusions and foolish toys that divide heart from
heart, and make man unmerciful to his brother !

It was not now to be hoped that the genius of Burns
would ever reach maturity, or accomplish aught worthy
of itself.   His spirit was jarred in its melody ; not the
soft breath of natural feeling, but the rude hand of Fate,
was now sweeping over the strings.   And yet what harmony was in him, what music even in his discords !   How
the wild tones had a charm for the simplest and the
wisest ; and all men felt and knew that here also was one
of the Gifted !   'If he entered an inn at midnight, after
all the inmates were in bed, the news of his arrival circu-
lated from the cellar to the garret ; and ere ten minutes
had elapsed, the landlord and all his guests were assem-
bled !'   Some brief pure moments of poetic life were yet
appointed him, in the composition of his Songs.   We
can understand how he grasped at this employment ; and
how too, he spurned all other reward for it but what the

---

[1] Tripping.

[2] *Ubi sæva indignatio cor ulterius lacerare nequit.*   Swift's Epitaph.

labour itself brought him. For the soul of Burns, though
scathed and marred, was yet living in its full moral
strength, though sharply conscious of its errors and
abasement : and here, in his destitution and degradation,
was one act of seeming nobleness and self-devotedness 5
left even for him to perform. He felt too, that with all
the 'thoughtless follies' that had 'laid him low,' the world
was unjust and cruel to him ; and he silently appealed
to another and calmer time. Not as a hired soldier,
but as a patriot, would he strive for the glory of his 10
country : so he cast from him the poor sixpence a day,
and served zealously as a volunteer. Let us not grudge
him this last luxury of his existence ; let him not have
appealed to us in vain ! The money was not necessary
to him ; he struggled through without it : long since, 15
these guineas would have been gone, and now the high-
mindedness of refusing them will plead for him in all
hearts forever.

We are here arrived at the crisis of Burns's life; for
matters had now taken such a shape with him as could 20
not long continue. If improvement was not to be looked
for, Nature could only for a limited time maintain this
dark and maddening warfare against the world and itself.
We are not medically informed whether any continuance
of years was, at this period, probable for Burns ; whether 25
his death is to be looked on as in some sense an acciden-
tal event, or only as the natural consequence of the long
series of events that had preceded. The latter seems to
be the likelier opinion ; and yet it is by no means a certain one. At all events, as we have said, *some* change 30
could not be very distant. Three gates of deliverance,
it seems to us, were open for Burns : clear poetical
activity ; madness ; or death. The first, with longer life,
was still possible, though not probable : for physical

causes were beginning to be concerned in it : and yet
Burns had an iron resolution ; could he but have seen
and felt, that not only his highest glory, but his first
duty, and the true medicine for all his woes, lay here.
5 The second was still less probable ; for his mind was
ever among the clearest and firmest. So the milder
third gate was opened for him : and he passed, not
softly yet speedily, into that still country, where the
hail-storms and fire-showers do not reach, and the heavi-
10 est-laden wayfarer at length lays down his load !

Contemplating this sad end of Burns, and how he
sank unaided by any real help, uncheered by any wise
sympathy, generous minds have sometimes figured to
themselves, with a reproachful sorrow, that much might
15 have been done for him ; that by counsel, true affection
and friendly ministrations, he might have been saved to
himself and the world. We question whether there is
not more tenderness of heart than soundness of judgment in these suggestions. It seems dubious to us
20 whether the richest, wisest, most benevolent individual
could have lent Burns any effectual help. Counsel,
which seldom profits any one, he did not need ; in his
understanding, he knew the right from the wrong, as
well perhaps as any man ever did ; but the persuasion,
25 which would have availed him, lies not so much in the
head as in the heart, where no argument or expostula-
tion could have assisted much to implant it. As to
money again, we do not believe that this was his essential want ; or well see how any private man could, even
30 presupposing Burns's consent, have bestowed on him an
independent fortune, with much prospect of decisive
advantage. It is a mortifying truth, that two men in
any rank of society, could hardly be found virtuous

enough to give money, and to take it as a necessary gift, without injury to the moral entireness of one or both. But so stands the fact : Friendship, in the old heroic sense of that term, no longer exists ; except in the cases of kindred or other legal affinity, it is in reality 5 no longer expected, or recognised as a virtue among men. A close observer of manners has pronounced 'Patronage,' that is, pecuniary or other economic further- ance, to be 'twice cursed'; cursing him that gives, and him that takes ! And thus, in regard to outward matters 10 also, it has become the rule, as in regard to inward it always was and must be the rule, that no one shall look for effectual help to another ; but that each shall rest contented with what help he can afford himself. Such, we say, is the principle of modern Honour ; naturally 15 enough growing out of that sentiment of Pride, which we inculcate and encourage as the basis of our whole social morality. Many a poet has been poorer than Burns ; but no one was ever prouder : we may question whether, without great precautions, even a pension from Royalty 20 would not have galled and encumbered, more than actually assisted him.

Still less, therefore, are we disposed to join with another class of Burns's admirers, who accuse the higher ranks among us of having ruined Burns by their selfish neglect 25 of him. We have already stated our doubts whether direct pecuniary help, had it been offered, would have been accepted, or could have proved very effectual. We shall readily admit, however, that much was to be done for Burns; that many a poisoned arrow might have been 30 warded from his bosom; many an entanglement in his path cut asunder by the hand of the powerful; and light and heat, shed on him from high places, would have made his humble atmosphere more genial ; and the soft-

est heart then breathing might have lived and died with
some fewer pangs. Nay, we shall grant farther, and for
Burns it is granting much, that, with all his pride, he
would have thanked, even with exaggerated gratitude, any
5 one who had cordially befriended him: patronage, unless
once cursed, needed not to have been twice so. At all
events, the poor promotion he desired in his calling might
have been granted : it was his own scheme, therefore
likelier than any other to be of service. All this it might
10 have been a luxury, nay it was a duty, for our nobility to
have done. No part of all this, however, did any of them
do; or apparently attempt, or wish to do : so much is
granted against them. But what then is the amount of
their blame ? Simply that they were men of the world,
15 and walked by the principles of such men ; that they
treated Burns, as other nobles and other commoners had
done other poets ; as the English did Shakspeare; as
King Charles and his Cavaliers did Butler, as King
Philip and his Grandees did Cervantes. Do men gather
20 grapes of thorns ; or shall we cut down our thorns for
yielding only a *fence* and haws ? How, indeed, could the
'nobility and gentry of his native land' hold out any help
to this 'Scottish Bard, proud of his name and country' ?
Were the nobility and gentry so much as able rightly
25 to help themselves ? Had they not their game to pre-
serve ; their borough interests to strengthen; dinners,
therefore, of various kinds to eat and give ? Were their
means more than adequate to all this business, or less than
adequate ? Less than adequate, in general; few of them
30 in reality were richer than Burns ; many of them were
poorer ; for sometimes they had to wring their supplies,
as with thumbscrews, from the hard hand; and, in their
need of guineas, to forget their duty of mercy ; which
Burns was never reduced to do. Let us pity and forgive

them. The game they preserved and shot, the dinners they ate and gave, the borough interests they strengthened, the *little* Babylons they severally builded by the glory of their might, are all melted or melting back into the primeval Chaos, as man's merely selfish endeavours are fated 5 to do : and here was an action, extending, in virtue of its worldly influence, we may say, through all time; in virtue of its moral nature, beyond all time, being immortal as the Spirit of Goodness itself; this action was offered them to do, and light was not given them to do it. Let us 10 pity and forgive them. But better than pity, let us go and *do otherwise.* Human suffering did not end with the life of Burns ; neither was the solemn mandate, ' Love one another, bear one another's burdens,' given to the rich only, but to all men. True, we shall find no Burns 15 to relieve, to assuage by our aid or our pity; but celestial natures, groaning under the fardels of a weary life, we shall still find ; and that wretchedness which Fate has rendered *voiceless* and *tuneless* is not the least wretched, but the most. 20

Still, we do not think that the blame of Burns's failure lies chiefly with the world. The world, it seems to us, treated him with more rather than with less kindness than it usually shows to such men. It has ever, we fear, shown but small favour to its Teachers: hunger and 25 nakedness, perils and revilings, the prison, the cross, the poison-chalice have, in most times and countries, been the market-price it has offered for Wisdom, the welcome with which it has greeted those who have come to enlighten and purify it. Homer and Socrates, and the Christian 30 Apostles, belong to old days ; but the world's Martyrology was not completed with these. Roger Bacon and Galileo languish in priestly dungeons; Tasso pines in the cell of a madhouse; Camoens dies begging on the streets of

Lisbon.   So neglected, so 'persecuted they the Prophets,' not in Judea only, but in all places where men have been. We reckon that every poet of Burns's order is, or should be, a prophet and teacher to his age ; that he has no
5 right to expect great kindness from it, but rather is bound to do it great kindness ; that Burns, in particular, experienced fully the usual proportion of the world's goodness ; and that the blame of his failure, as we have said, lies not chiefly with the world.

10   Where, then, does it lie?   We are forced to answer : With himself ; it is his inward, not his outward misfortunes that bring him to the dust.   Seldom, indeed, is it otherwise ; seldom is a life morally wrecked but the grand cause lies in some internal mal-arrangement, some want
15 less of good fortune than of good guidance.   Nature fashions no creature without implanting in it the strength needful for its action and duration ; least of all does she so neglect her masterpiece and darling, the poetic soul. Neither can we believe that it is in the power of *any* ex-
20 ternal circumstances utterly to ruin the mind of a man ; nay if proper wisdom be given him, even so much as to affect its essential health and beauty.   The sternest sum-total of all worldly misfortunes is Death ; nothing more *can* lie in the cup of human woe : yet many men, in all
25 ages, have triumphed over Death, and led it captive ; converting its physical victory into a moral victory for themselves, into a real and immortal consecration for all that their past life had achieved.   What has been done, may be done again : nay, it is but the degree and not the
30 kind of such heroism that differs in different seasons ; for without some portion of this spirit, not of boisterous daring, but of silent fearlessness, of Self-denial in all its forms, no good man, in any scene or time, has ever attained to be good.

We have already stated the error of Burns; and mourned over it, rather than blamed it. It was the want of unity in his purposes, of consistency in his aims; the hapless attempt to mingle in friendly union the common spirit of the world with the spirit of poetry, which is of a far different and altogether irreconcilable nature. Burns was nothing wholly, and Burns could be nothing, no man formed as he was can be anything, by halves. The heart, not of a mere hot-blooded, popular Versemonger, or poetical *Restaurateur*, but of a true Poet and Singer, worthy of the old religious heroic times, had been given him: and he fell in an age, not of heroism and religion, but of scepticism, selfishness and triviality, when true Nobleness was little understood, and its place supplied by a hollow, dissocial, altogether barren and unfruitful principle of Pride. The influences of that age, his open, kind, susceptible nature, to say nothing of his highly untoward situation, made it more than usually difficult for him to cast aside, or rightly subordinate; the better spirit that was within him ever sternly demanded its rights, its supremacy: he spent his life in endeavouring to reconcile these two; and lost it, as he must lose it, without reconciling them.

Burns was born poor; and born also to continue poor, for he would not endeavour to be otherwise: this it had been well could he have once for all admitted, and considered as finally settled. He was poor, truly; but hundreds even of his own class and order of minds have been poorer, yet have suffered nothing deadly from it: nay, his own Father had a far sorer battle with ungrateful destiny than his was; and he did not yield to it, but died courageously warring, and to all moral intents prevailing, against it. True, Burns had little means, had even little time for poetry, his only real pursuit and vocation; but

so much the more precious was what little he had.   In all
these external respects his case was hard ; but very far
from the hardest.   Poverty, incessant drudgery and much
worse evils, it has often been the lot of Poets and wise
5 men to strive with, and their glory to conquer.   Locke
was banished as a traitor ; and wrote his *Essay on the
Human Understanding* sheltering himself in a Dutch garret.   Was Milton rich or at his ease when he composed
Paradise Lost ?   Not only low, but fallen from a height ;
10 not only poor, but impoverished ; in darkness and with
dangers compassed round, he sang his immortal song,
and found fit audience, though few.   Did not Cervantes
finish his work, a maimed soldier and in prison ?   Nay,
was not the *Araucana*, which Spain acknowledges as its
15 Epic, written without even the aid of paper ; on scraps
of leather, as the stout fighter and voyager snatched any
moment from that wild warfare ?

And what, then, had these men, which Burns wanted ?
Two things ; both which, it seems to us, are indispen-
20 sable for such men.   They had a true, religious principle
of morals ; and a single, not a double aim in their activity.
They were not self-seekers and self-worshippers ; but
seekers and worshippers of something far better than Self.
Not personal enjoyment was their object ; but a high,
25 heroic idea of Religion, of Patriotism, of heavenly Wisdom, in one or the other form, ever hovered before them ;
in which cause they neither shrank from suffering, nor
called on the earth to witness it as something wonderful ;
but patiently endured, counting it blessedness enough so
30 to spend and be spent.   Thus the 'golden-calf of Self-
love,' however curiously carved, was not their Deity ;
but the Invisible Goodness, which alone is man's reason-
able service.   This feeling was as a celestial fountain,
whose streams refreshed into gladness and beauty all the

provinces of their otherwise too desolate existence. In a word, they willed one thing, to which all other things were subordinated and made subservient ; and therefore they accomplished it. The wedge will rend rocks; but its edge must be sharp and single : if it be double, the wedge is bruised in pieces and will rend nothing.

Part of this superiority these men owed to their age ; in which heroism and devotedness were still practised, or at least not yet disbelieved in : but much of it likewise they owed to themselves. With Burns, again, it was different. His morality, in most of its practical points, is that of a mere worldly man; enjoyment, in a finer or coarser shape, is the only thing he longs and strives for. A noble instinct sometimes raises him above this ; but an instinct only, and acting only for moments. He has no Religion ; in the shallow age, where his days were cast, Religion was not discriminated from the New and Old Light *forms* of Religion ; and was, with these, becoming obsolete in the minds of men. His heart, indeed, is alive with a trembling adoration, but there is no temple in his understanding. He lives in darkness and in the shadow of doubt. His religion, at best, is an anxious wish; like that of Rabelais, 'a great Perhaps.'

He loved Poetry warmly, and in his heart; could he but have loved it purely, and with his whole undivided heart, it had been well. For Poetry, as Burns could have followed it, is but another form of Wisdom, of Religion; is itself Wisdom and Religion. But this also was denied him. His poetry is a stray vagrant gleam, which will not be extinguished within him, yet rises not to be the true light of his path, but is often a wildfire that misleads him. It was not necessary for Burns to be rich, to be, or to seem, 'independent' ; but it *was* necessary for him to be at one with his own heart; to place what was highest in his nature highest also in his life; 'to seek within himself for that consistency and sequence, which external events would forever refuse him.' He was born a poet; poetry was the celestial element of his being, and should have been

5 the soul of his whole endeavours. Lifted into that serene ether, whither he had wings given him to mount, he would have needed no other elevation: poverty, neglect and all evil, save the desecration of himself and his Art, were a small matter to him; the pride and the passions

10 of the world lay far beneath his feet; and he looked down alike on noble and slave, on prince and beggar, and all that wore the stamp of man, with clear recognition, with brotherly affection, with sympathy, with pity. Nay, we question whether for his culture as a Poet poverty and

15 much suffering for a season were not absolutely advantageous. Great men, in looking back over their lives, have testified to that effect. 'I would not for much,' says Jean Paul, 'that I had been born richer.' And yet Paul's birth was poor enough; for, in another place, he adds:

20 'The prisoner's allowance is bread and water; and I had often only the latter.' But the gold that is refined in the hottest furnace comes out the purest; or, as he has himself expressed it, 'the canary-bird sings sweeter the longer it has been trained in a darkened cage.'

25 A man like Burns might have divided his hours between poetry and virtuous industry; industry which all true feeling sanctions, nay prescribes, and which has a beauty, for that cause, beyond the pomp of thrones: but to divide his hours between poetry and rich men's

30 banquets was an ill-starred and inauspicious attempt. How could he be at ease at such banquets? What had he to do there, mingling his music with the coarse roar of altogether earthly voices; brightening the thick smoke of intoxication with fire lent him from heaven? Was it his

aim to *enjoy* life? Tomorrow he must go drudge as an Exciseman! We wonder not that Burns became moody, indignant, and at times an offender against certain rules of society; but rather that he did not grow utterly frantic, and ran *amuck* against them all. How could a man, so 5 falsely placed by his own or others' fault, ever know contentment or peaceable diligence for an hour? What he did, under such perverse guidance, and what he forbore to do, alike fill us with astonishment at the natural strength and worth of his character. 10

Doubtless there was a remedy for this perverseness; but not in others; only in himself; least of all in simple increase of wealth and worldly 'respectability.' We hope we have now heard enough about the efficacy of wealth for poetry, and to make poets happy. Nay have we not 15 seen another instance of it in these very days? Byron, a man of an endowment considerably less ethereal than that of Burns, is born in the rank not of a Scottish ploughman, but of an English peer: the highest worldly honours, the fairest worldly career, are his by inheritance; the richest 20 harvest of fame he soon reaps, in another province, by his own hand. And what does all this avail him? Is he happy, is he good, is he true? Alas, he has a poet's soul, and strives towards the Infinite and the Eternal; and soon feels that all this is but mounting to the house-top to 25 reach the stars! Like Burns, he is only a proud man; might, like him, have 'purchased a pocket-copy of Milton to study the character of Satan'; for Satan also is Byron's grand exemplar, the hero of his poetry, and the model apparently of his conduct. As in Burns's case too, the 30 celestial element will not mingle with the clay of earth; both poet and man of the world he must not be; vulgar Ambition will not live kindly with poetic Adoration; he *cannot* serve God and Mammon. Byron, like Burns, is

not happy; nay he is the most wretched of all men. His
life is falsely arranged: the fire that is in him is not a
strong, still, central fire, warming into beauty the products
of a world; but it is the mad fire of a volcano; and now
5 — we look sadly into the ashes of a crater, which ere long
will fill itself with snow !

Byron and Burns were sent forth as missionaries to
their generation, to teach it a higher Doctrine, a purer
Truth; they had a message to deliver, which left them no
10 rest till it was accomplished; in dim throes of pain, this
divine behest lay smouldering within them; for they knew
not what it meant, and felt it only in mysterious anticipation, and they had to die without articulately uttering it.
They are in the camp of the Unconverted; yet not as high
15 messengers of rigorous though benignant truth, but as
soft flattering singers, and in pleasant fellowship will they
live there: they are first adulated, then persecuted; they
accomplish little for others; they find no peace for themselves, but only death and the peace of the grave. We
20 confess, it is not without a certain mournful awe that we
view the fate of these noble souls, so richly gifted, yet
ruined to so little purpose with all their gifts. It seems
to us there is a stern moral taught in this piece of history,
— *twice* told us in our own time ! Surely to men of like
25 genius, if there be any such, it carries with it a lesson of
deep impressive significance. Surely it would become
such a man, furnished for the highest of all enterprises,
that of being the Poet of his Age, to consider well what
it is that he attempts, and in what spirit he attempts it.
30 For the words of Milton are true in all times, and were
never truer than in this: 'He who would write heroic
poems must make his whole life a heroic poem.' If he
cannot first so make his life, then let him hasten from
this arena; for neither its lofty glories, nor its fearful

perils, are fit for him. Let him dwindle into a modish balladmonger; let him worship and besing the idols of the time, and the time will not fail to reward him. If, indeed, he can endure to live in that capacity! Byron and Burns could not live as idol-priests, but the fire of their own hearts consumed them; and better it was for them that they could not. For it is not in the favour of the great or of the small, but in a life of truth, and in the inexpugnable citadel of his own soul, that a Byron's or a Burns's strength must lie. Let the great stand aloof from him, or know how to reverence him. Beautiful is the union of wealth with favour and furtherance for litera- ture; like the costliest flower-jar enclosing the loveliest amaranth. Yet let not the relation be mistaken. A true poet is not one whom they can hire by money or flattery to be a minister of their pleasures, their writer of occasional verses, their purveyor of table-wit; he cannot be their men- ial, he cannot even be their partisan. At the peril of both parties, let no such union be attempted! Will a Courser of the Sun work softly in the harness of a Dray-horse? His hoofs are of fire, and his path is through the heavens, bringing light to all lands; will he lumber on mud high- ways, dragging ale for earthly appetites from door to door?

But we must stop short in these considerations, which would lead us to boundless lengths. We had something to say on the public moral character of Burns; but this also we must forbear. We are far from regarding him as guilty before the world, as guiltier than the average; nay from doubting that he is less guilty than one of ten thou- sand. Tried at a tribunal far more rigid than that where the *Plebiscita* of common civic reputations are pronounced, he has seemed to us even there less worthy of blame than of pity and wonder. But the world is habitually unjust in its judgments of such men; unjust on many grounds,

of which this one may be stated as the substance: It
decides, like a court of law, by dead statutes; and not
positively but negatively, less on what is done right, than
on what is or is not done wrong. Not the few inches of
5 deflection from the mathematical orbit, which are so easily
measured, but the *ratio* of these to the whole diameter,
constitutes the real aberration. This orbit may be a
planet's, its diameter the breadth of the solar system; or
it may be a city hippodrome; nay the circle of a ginhorse,
10 its diameter a score of feet or paces. But the inches of
deflection only are measured: and it is assumed that the
diameter of the ginhorse, and that of the planet, will yield
the same ratio when compared with them! Here lies the
root of many a blind, cruel condemnation of Burnses,
15 Swifts, Rousseaus, which one never listens to with ap-
proval. Granted, the ship comes into harbour with shrouds
and tackle damaged; the pilot is blameworthy; he has not
been all-wise and all-powerful: but to know *how* blameworthy, tell us first whether his voyage has been round
20 the Globe, or only to Ramsgate and the Isle of Dogs.

With our readers in general, with men of right feeling
anywhere, we are not required to plead for Burns. In
pitying admiration he lies enshrined in all our hearts, in
a far nobler mausoleum than that one of marble; neither
25 will his Works, even as they are, pass away from the
memory of men. While the Shakspeares and Miltons
roll on like mighty rivers through the country of Thought,
bearing fleets of traffickers and assiduous pearl-fishers on
their waves; this little Valclusa Fountain will also arrest
30 our eye: for this also is of Nature's own and most cunning workmanship, bursts from the depths of the earth,
with a full gushing current, into the light of day; and
often will the traveller turn aside to drink of its clear
waters, and muse among its rocks and pines!

NOTES.

————◆————

1 2. **Butler.** Are there not good reasons why the author of *Hudibras* should not have expected to be a general favorite?

1 15. **brave mausoleum.** At Dumfries, where Burns spent the last five years of his life. In it were buried the poet, his wife and children.

In 1820 the foundation stone was laid for the monument on Alloway Croft, near the Auld Brig of Doon. £3300 was subscribed for this purpose.

Eleven years later work began on the Edinburgh monument, which cost even more.

There are statues of Burns in Glasgow, Kilmarnock, New York, Dundee, Dumfries, London, Albany (N.Y.), Ayr, Aberdeen, Irvine, Paisley, Chicago, and other places.

2 12. **Lucy's.** It was in Lucy's park, says tradition, that Shakspere did his deer-stealing. On evidence of equal value is based the legend which names him as the author of a doggerel epitaph on John à Combe.

2 22. **Excise Commissioners.** Cf. p. 10, ll. 27–30.

2 22. **Gentlemen of the Caledonian Hunt.** A company of Scottish noblemen and gentry interested in field sports. They allowed Burns to dedicate to them the second edition of his poems, and subscribed individually for copies. Directly and indirectly, the members of this aristocratic association were very helpful to the young poet.

2 23. **Dumfries Aristocracy.** Dumfries, "a great stage on the road from England to Ireland," was a small provincial town notable for its public entertainments. The Caledonian Hunt sometimes met there; the country gentlemen often. Parties of strangers would send for Burns, "the standing marvel of the place," and he weakly went to amuse them with his jokes, toasts, and songs.

2 25. **New and Old Light Clergy.** The New Lights were more liberal, more progressive than the Old Lights. The two factions of the Church were at sword's points. Burns naturally sympathized with the New Lights.

4 3. **Constable's Miscellany.** Constable was a well-known Edinburgh publisher. *Lockhart's Life* came out in April, 1828. The whole impression was exhausted in six weeks. Before the end of the year Carlyle's review of Lockhart's volume had "raised the enthusiasm of the world on the subject."

4 13. **Mr. Morris Birkbeck,** author of *Notes on a Journey in America. from the Coast of Virginia to the Territory of Illinois,* 2d ed., London. 1818.

6 10. **An educated man.** Contrast with this short life Milton's period of preparation for writing. It has been said that the noble mind needs abundant leisure.

6 26. **Condition the most disadvantageous.** Cf. p. 66, ll. 13 ff. "Nay, we question whether for his culture as a Poet poverty and much suffering for a season were not absolutely advantageous," etc.

6 31. **Ferguson or Ramsay.** Ramsay, who died about a year before Burns was born, has been called the most famous Scottish poet of the period. *The Gentle Shepherd* was a classic to the people. Burns, in writing of "the excellent Ramsay and the still more excellent Ferguson," shows better judgment than most of the critics, according to Professor Hugh Walker and Mr. Wallace. These Scottish poets and their followers broke away from the traditions of the 'correct' poets and practiced "much of what is best in Wordsworth's doctrine of poetic diction and of the proper subjects for poetic treatment."

Burns imitated Ferguson oftener than any other poet. Burns never forgot his obligations to Ferguson. He writes : "Rhyme I had given up [on going to Irvine], but, meeting with Ferguson's *Scottish Poems*, I strung anew my wildly sounding lyre with emulating vigour." And in raising a simple monument to the memory of Ferguson, he honored what was probably up to this point "the best expression of the spirit which animated himself."

7 25. **Criticism . . . a cold business.** The world still needs sympathetic critics. Cf. Dr. Henry Van Dyke's *The Poetry of Tennyson,* a fine specimen of literary appreciation. Cf. also Matthew Arnold's theory of criticism.

10 25. **Æolian harp.** Ruskin says he knows no poetry so sorrowful as Scott's. "Scott is inherently and consistently sad. Around all his power and brightness and enjoyment of eye and heart, the far-away Æolian knell is forever sounding."

10 30. **gauging ale barrels!** "The excise scheme was a pet one of the bard's own, and consideration of that fact ought to have checked the indignant utterances of Carlyle and others of smaller note who

declaimed against his friendly patrons for finding no better post for him than ' a Gaugership.' " — W. S. Douglas.

12 18. **Si vis me flere.**

> Si vis me flere, dolendum est
> primum ipsi tibi.
> — Horace: *De Arte Poetica Liber*, ll. 102, 103.

"If you would have me weep, you yourself must first know sorrow."

15 21. **Mrs. Dunlop.** During a period of depression Mrs. Dunlop, a wealthy woman of high rank, happened to read *The Cotter's Saturday Night*. The faithful, simple description charmed her back to her normal condition. Her interest in this poem was the beginning of a correspondence that lasted as long as Burns lived. Of all his friendships, says Gilbert Burns, "none seemed more agreeable to him than that of Mrs. Dunlop." Naturally enough, letters written to such a friend furnish very interesting material for the poet's biography.

17 17. **a vates.** The function of "legislators, prophets, philosophers, poets . . . is always the same, to call back to nature and truth the spoiled children of convention and affectation. Of these messengers, the most wide in his range, and most generally accepted, is the poet ; for, while the legislator is often cramped by the hardness of the materials with which he has to deal, and the prophet too often has his influence confined and bound by the very forms of a church which owed its existence, perhaps, to his catholicity, the great poet in his honest utterances is hampered by no forces external to his own genius.

"The works of such great poets — for we do not speak here of mere dressers of pretty fancies — are a real evangel of Nature to all people who have ears to hear. Such men were Homer and Pindar to the Greeks ; Horace and Virgil to the Romans ; to the English, Shakspere and Wordsworth ; to Scotland, Walter Scott and Robert Burns." — Blackie.

17 24. **Minerva Press.** A London press, noted in the eighteenth century for turning out sentimental novels.

18 14. **Borgia.** Although Macchiavelli in his " Principe " represents this skillful politician as a model ruler, the name still stands for cruelty and treachery.

18 17. **Mossgiel and Tarbolton.** See *Outline of the Life of Burns.*

18 19. **Crockford's.** A famous gaming club-house in London.

20 15. **Retzsch.** A German etcher and painter, famous for his etchings illustrating works of Goethe, Schiller, and Shakspere.

22 11. **Clearness of Sight.** Ruskin says: "The greatest thing a human soul ever does in this world is to *see* something, and tell what it *saw* in a plain way. Hundreds of people can talk for one who can think, but thousands can think for one who can see. To see clearly is poetry, prophecy, and religion, — all in one."

"The world of Literature is more or less divided into Thinkers and Seers. . . . I believe . . . the Seers are wholly the greater race of the two."

"A true Thinker, who has practical purpose in his thinking, and is sincere, as Plato or Carlyle or Helps, becomes in some sort a seer, and must be always of infinite use in his generation." — RUSKIN on Scott, *Modern Painters*, vol. III, part iv, "Of Many Things."

23 6. **red-wat-shod.** Wat means wet.

23 23. **Keats.** Is Carlyle's criticism of Keats appreciative?

24 3. **Novum Organum.** One of Bacon's scientific works. Macaulay says: "The *Novum Organum* and the *De Augmentis* are much talked of, but little read. They have produced, indeed, a vast effect on the opinions of mankind; but they have produced it through the operation of intermediate agents. They have moved the intellects which have moved the world."

27 12. **Dr. Slop.** Carlyle quotes from Sterne's *Tristram Shandy*, a book which Burns "devoured at meals, spoon in hand."

28 20. **Scots wha hae wi' Wallace bled.** Mr. Quiller Couch says that *Bannockburn* seems to him to be rant; "very fine rant — inspired rant, if you will — hovering on the borders of poetry."

Mr. Wallace says: "Under cover of a fourteenth century battle-song he [Burns] was really liberating his soul against the Tory tyranny that was opposing liberty at home and abroad, and, moreover, striking at the comfort of his own fireside."

29 5. **Cacus.** A giant.

31 1. **Tieck . . . Musäus.** Each of these Germans wrote German folk tales. The chief note of those of Musäus is said to be their artificial naïveté. Yet the "satirical humour, quaint fancy, and graceful writing" have made them a classic of their kind.

31 16. **Tam o' Shanter.** Both Lockhart and Cunningham give some account of the day on which Burns wrote the poem which he considered his masterpiece. Principal Shairp also tells the story in his *Robert Burns*, p. 121.

Scott had *Tam o' Shanter* in mind when he said that "no poet, with the exception of Shakspere, ever possessed the power of exciting the most varied and discordant emotions with such rapid transitions."

31 34. ' **Poosie Nansie.** ' It was in her alehouse that the *raucle carlin* (fearless crone), the *wee Apollo*, the *Son of Mars*, and the others met for their good time.

32 21. Beggars' Opera. An eighteenth-century production by John Gay. He transforms a motley company of highwaymen, pickpockets, etc., into a group of fine gentlemen and ladies in order to satirize the corrupt political conditions of the time.

Beggars' Bush. A seventeenth-century work by John Fletcher and others.

32 28. his Songs. Emerson said the reason why the great English race, all over the world, honored the poet as it did on the hundredth anniversary of his birth was because "Robert Burns, the poet of the middle class, represents in the mind of men to-day that great uprising of the middle class against the armed and privileged minorities, that uprising which worked politically in the American and French Revolutions, and which, not in governments so much as in education and social order, has changed the face of the world. . . . The Confession of Augsburg, the Declaration of Independence, the French Rights of Man, and the ' Marseillaise ' are not more weighty documents in the history of freedom than the songs of Burns."

33 12. Ossorius (Osorio). Bacon comments on the tendency of this man to sacrifice substance to style. A philosophical writer, his chief work is a Latin history of the reign of Emanuel I.

34 27. our Fletcher's aphorism. Andrew Fletcher, a famous Scottish patriot. For a short account of the man, and an exact quotation of the saying that has made him famous, see *Chambers's Encyclopædia*.

35 21. Grays and Glovers. Why does Carlyle mention Glover in connection with Gray? Stopford Brooke says, "The ' Elegy ' will always remain one of the beloved poems of Englishmen. It is not only a piece of exquisite work ; it is steeped in England."

36 3. Boston (Thomas). Carlyle mentions the best-known work of this Scotch Presbyterian divine. His influence as a Calvinistic theologian is said to have affected several generations of Scottish people.

36 29. La Flèche. A town in France where the famous Scottish philosopher and historian, David Hume, spent three years. He describes himself as wandering about there "in solitude, and dreaming the dream of his philosophy."

41 4. Mossgiel. The town in which Burns did most of his best work.

45 11. **character for sobriety . . . destroyed.** Burns was then living at Mossgiel. During these years, his brother Gilbert says, "his temperance and frugality were everything that could be desired." Mr. Scott Douglas adds: "The effect of prevalent misconception on this point is visible, even in Mr. Carlyle's in many respects incomparable essay. The poet had at Kirkoswald and Irvine learned to drink, and he was all his life liable to social excesses, but it is unfair to say that his 'character for sobriety was destroyed.'"

46 11. **a mad Rienzi.** A Roman political reformer of the fourteenth century. "The nobles never acknowledged his government . . . and the populace became so infuriated by his arbitrary measures that a crowd surrounded him on the stairs of the Capitol and killed him."

47 20. **Virgilium vidi tantum.** I have caught a glimpse of Virgil.

48 23. **Mr. Nasmyth's picture.** See *Life and Works of Robert Burns* by Dr. Robert Chambers, 1896 edition, by William Wallace, vol. II, p. 55, for an engraving from this portrait.

49 23. **in malem partem,** disparagingly.

50 34. **good old Blacklock.** Burns says: "Dr. Blacklock belonged to a set of critics for whose *applause* I had not *dared to hope.*" Dr. Thomas Blacklock, of Edinburgh, was a blind poet, of whom Dr. Johnson wrote that he "looked on him with reverence." [Letter to Mrs. Thrale, Edinburgh, August 17, 1773.] Upon hearing Burns's poems read he wrote an appreciative letter to their common friend Dr. Lawrie, urging that a second edition be printed at once. Burns says: "Dr. Blacklock's idea that I should meet every encouragement for a second edition fired me so much that away I posted to Edinburgh."

51 27. **Excise and Farm scheme.** Burns felt compelled to undertake the excise work in order to eke out the scanty income his farm yielded.

52 5. **preferred self help.** "Burns, however, asked nothing from his Edinburgh friends ; when they helped him to a farm and a position in the Excise, believing, as they apparently did, that they were thereby gratifying his own wishes, he made no complaint, but cheerfully prepared himself for the necessarily uncongenial career which alone appeared open to him." — WILLIAM WALLACE'S *Life.*

53 9. **Mæcenas.** The friend and patron of Horace and Virgil.

54 21. **collision with . . . Superiors.** Burns writes: "I have been surprised, confounded, and distracted by Mr. Mitchell, the Collector, telling me that he has received an order from your Board [the Scottish Board of Excise] to inquire into my political conduct, and blaming me as a person disaffected to Government." But it seems clear that he was not very severely reprimanded at headquarters, because later in this same year the official record is, " The Poet; does pretty well."

Cf. "The Deil's Awa Wi' Th' Exciseman," and the story of the circumstances under which it was written.

55 8. **Dumfries Aristocracy.** " If there is any truth in the story, on which so much false sentiment has been wasted, about Burns walking the shady side of the street while the Dumfries gentry on the other side would not recognise him, it proves at all events that Burns knew no reason why he should not show himself on the street as well as the proudest among them." — WALLACE.

In January, 1794, "about the time usually selected for his final surrender to the drink-fiend," Burns wrote : 'Some . . . have conceived a prejudice against me as being a drunken, dissipated character. I might be all this, you know, and yet be an honest fellow; but you know that I am an honest fellow and am nothing of this.'

57 12. **a volunteer.** In 1795, while a large part of the regular army was fighting against France abroad, Dumfries raised two companies of volunteers. Among the liberals, against whom severe accusations had been made, and who welcomed this opportunity to show their loyalty, was Burns. Cunningham says he well remembers the swarthy, stooping ploughman handling his arms with "indifferent dexterity " in this respectable and picturesque corps. As a further indication of the poet's feeling he wrote *The Dumfries Volunteers*, a ballad that first appeared in the *Dumfries Journal* and was at once reprinted in other newspapers and magazines.

60 7. **promotion.** To escape the "incessant drudgery " of the Supervisorship, Burns wanted to be the Excise Collector. He thought this position would give him " a decent competence " and " a life of literary leisure." He would ask for nothing more.

Butler. Cf. p. 1.

61 32. **Roger Bacon.** His *Opus Majus* ("Greater Work ") is, to borrow the phrase of Dr. Whewell, " at once the *Encyclopædia* and the *Novum Organum* of the thirteenth century." " 'Unheard, forgotten, buried,' the old man died as he had lived, and it has been reserved for later ages to roll away the obscurity that had gathered round his memory, and to place first in the great roll of modern science the name of Roger Bacon." — J. R. GREEN, *Short History of the English People*, p. 141. See *Novum Organum*, p. 24 of this essay, and the note.

61 33. **Tasso pines in the cell of a madhouse.** During these seven years of confinement his greatest work was read all over Europe. It is said that he is the last Italian poet whose influence made itself felt

throughout Europe, and that his *Jerusalem* is the "culminating poetical product" of the sixteenth century, as Dante's *Divine Comedy* is of the fourteenth.

61 34. **Camoens.** A celebrated Portuguese poet of the sixteenth century.

64 14. **Araucana.** By Alonso de Ercilla.

65 15. **He has no Religion.** Carlyle did a great deal of vigorous thinking on the subject of religion. "A man's religion," he says, "is the chief fact with regard to him. . . . The thing a man does practically believe (and this is often enough *without* asserting it even to himself, much less to others); the thing a man does practically lay to heart, and know for certain concerning his vital relations to this mysterious Universe, and his duty and destiny there, that is in all cases the primary thing for him, and creatively determines all the rest. That is his religion; or, it may be, his mere scepticism and no-religion." Again Carlyle says of the man who has a religion: "Hourly and daily, for himself and for the whole world, a faithful, unspoken, but not ineffectual prayer rises: 'Thy will be done.' His whole work on earth is an emblematic spoken or acted prayer: 'Be the will of God done on Earth —not the Devil's will or any of the Devil's servants' wills!' . . . He has a religion, this man; an everlasting Load-star that beams the brighter in the Heavens, the darker here on Earth grows the night around him."

These citations may help us decide what Carlyle meant by saying that Burns had no religion. We are glad to have him add: "His religion, at best, is an anxious wish; like that of Rabelais, 'a great Perhaps.'" Some of us may agree with Professor Hugh Walker that there is only a half-truth in this concession, and that "Carlyle, in most respects so appreciative and so keen-sighted, is surely in error when he says that Burns had no religion." We can hardly escape the conclusion that Burns was at times strongly influenced by his religious hope. There are passages in several of his poems that we must not disregard; and in his letters he sometimes throws light on his religious views. For example, in a letter to Mrs. Dunlop, 1788, he writes: "Some things in your late letters hurt me; not that *you say them*, but that *you mistake me.* Religion, my honored madam, has not only been all my life my chief dependence, but my dearest enjoyment. I have indeed been the luckless victim of wayward follies; but, alas! I have ever been 'more fool than knave.' A mathematician without religion is a probable character; an irreligious poet is a monster." Some two years earlier he had written: "O, thou great unknown Power! Thou Almighty

God! who hast lighted up reason in my breast, and blessed me with immortality! I have frequently wandered from that order and regularity necessary for the perfection of thy works, yet thou hast never left me nor forsaken me!"

70 20. **Ramsgate.** A seaport in Kent, sixty-five miles from London.

70 20. **Isle of Dogs.** A peninsula on the bank of the Thames, opposite Greenwich.

70 29. **Valclusa.** Valcluse, near Avignon, was the quiet country home of

> " Fraunceys Petrark, . . . whose rethorike swete
> Enlumined al Itaille of poetrye."

CARLYLE'S SUMMARY.

—◆◆—

OUR grand maxim of supply and demand. Living misery and post-humous glory. The character of Burns a theme that cannot easily become exhausted. His Biographers. Perfection in Biography. — Burns one of the most considerable British men of the eighteenth century: an age the most prosaic Britain had yet seen. His hard and most dis-advantageous conditions. Not merely as a Poet, but as a Man, that he chiefly interests and affects us. His life a deeper tragedy than any brawling Napoleon's. His heart, erring and at length broken, full of inborn riches, of love to all living and lifeless things. The Peasant Poet bears himself among the low, with whom his lot is cast, like a King in exile. — His Writings but a poor mutilated fraction of what was in him, yet of a quality enduring as the English tongue. He wrote, not from hearsay, but from sight and actual experience. This, easy as it looks, the fundamental difficulty which all poets have to strive with. Byron, heartily as he detested insincerity, far enough from faultless. No poet of Burns's susceptibility from first to last so totally free from affectation. Some of his Letters, however, by no means deserve this praise. His singular power of making all subjects, even the most homely, interesting. Wherever there is a sky above him, and a world around him, the poet is in his place. Every genius an impossibility till he appears. — Burns's rugged earnest truth, yet tenderness and sweet native grace. His clear, graphic 'descriptive touches' and piercing emphasis of thought. Professor Stewart's testimony to Burns's intel-lectual vigour. A deeper insight than any 'doctrine of association.' In the Poetry of Burns keenness of insight keeps pace with keenness of feeling. Loving Indignation and *good* Hatred : *Scots wha hae ; Mac-pherson's Farewell :* Sunny buoyant floods of Humour. — Imperfections of Burns's poetry : *Tam o' Shanter*, not a true poem so much as a piece of sparkling rhetoric : The *Jolly Beggars*, the most complete and perfect as a poetical composition. His Songs the most truly inspired and most deeply felt of all his poems. His influence on the hearts and literature of his country : Literary patriotism. — Burns's acted Works even more interesting than his written ones ; and these too, alas, but a fragment :

His passionate youth never passed into clear and steadfast manhood. The only true happiness of a man : Often it is the greatest minds that are latest in obtaining it : Burns and Byron. Burns's hard-worked, yet happy boyhood: His estimable parents. Early dissipations. In Necessity and Obedience a man should find his highest Freedom. — Religious quarrels and scepticisms. Faithlessness : Exile and blackest desperation. Invited to Edinburgh : A Napoleon among the crowned sovereigns of Literature. Sir Walter Scott's reminiscence of an interview with Burns. Burns's calm, manly bearing amongst the Edinburgh aristocracy. His bitter feeling of his own indigence. By the great he is treated in the customary fashion ; and each party goes his several way. — What Burns was next to do, or to avoid : His Excise-and-Farm scheme not an unreasonable one : No failure of external means, but of internal, that overtook Burns. Good beginnings. Patrons of genius and picturesque tourists : Their moral rottenness, by which he became infected, gradually eat out the heart of his life. Meteors of French Politics rise before him, but they are not *his* stars. Calumny is busy with him. The little great-folk of Dumfries : Burns's desolation. In his destitution and degradation one act of self-devotedness still open to him : Not as a hired soldier, but as a patriot, would he strive for the glory of his country. The crisis of his life : Death. — Little effectual help could perhaps have been rendered to Burns : Patronage twice cursed : Many a poet has been poorer, none prouder. And yet much might have been done to have made his humble atmosphere more genial. Little Babylons and Babylonians : Let us go and *do otherwise*. The market-price of Wisdom. Not in the power of *any* mere external circumstances to ruin the mind of a man. The errors of Burns to be mourned over, rather than blamed. The great want of his life was the great want of his age, a true faith in Religion and a singleness and unselfishness of aim. — Poetry, as Burns could and ought to have followed it, is but another form of Wisdom, of Religion. For his culture as a Poet, poverty and much suffering for a season were absolutely advantageous. To divide his hours between poetry and rich men's banquets an ill-starred attempt. Byron, rich in worldly means and honours, no whit happier than Burns in his poverty and worldly degradation : They had a message from on High to deliver, which could leave them no rest while it remained unaccomplished. Death and the rest of the grave : A stern moral, *twice* told us in our own time. The world habitually unjust in its judgments of such men. With men of right feeling anywhere, there will be no need to plead for Burns : In pitying admiration he lies enshrined in all our hearts.

REFERENCE BOOKS.

———◆———

BURNS.

ARNOLD, MATTHEW. The Study of Poetry. (Essays in Criticism.)

BLACKIE, J. S. Life of Burns. (Great Writers.)

BLACKIE, J. S. Scottish Song.

BROOKE, STOPFORD. Theology in the English Poets.

BRUCE, WALLACE. The Land of Burns.

CARLYLE, THOMAS. Hero as Poet, and Hero as Man of Letters.

CUTHBERTSON, JOHN. Complete Glossary to the Poetry and Prose of Robert Burns.

DOUGLAS, W. S. Works of Robert Burns, Paterson edition, 6 vols. (with a Summary of his Career and Genius).

DOW, J. G. Selections from Burns. (Introduction, notes, and glossary.)

FERGUSON, R. Poems.

GEORGE, A. J. Select Poems of Burns (arranged chronologically, with notes).

GILES, H. Illustrations of Genius.

GRAHAM, P. ANDERSON. Nature in Books. (The Poetry of Toil— Burns.)

HALIBURTON, HUGH. Furth in Field.

HENLEY, W. E., and HENDERSON, T. F. The Poetry of Robert Burns. Centenary edition. 3 vols., with notes. Reprinted, 1 vol., in "The Cambridge Edition."

KINGSLEY, CHARLES. Burns and His School.

NICHOL, JOHN. Burns. (Encyclopædia Britannica.)

RAMSAY, A. Poems.

REID, J. B. Complete Concordance to the Poems and Songs of Robert Burns.

ROBERTSON, L. Selections from Burns. (Notes and glossary.)

ROSS, J. D. Round Burns' Grave : Pæans and Dirges of Many Bards (including Longfellow, Holmes, Whittier, Lowell, and Wordsworth).

Ross, J. D.   Burnsiana.

Setoun, Gabriel.   Robert Burns.   (Famous Scots Series.)

Shairp, J. C.   Robert Burns.   (English Men of Letters.)

Shairp, J. C.   Scottish Song and Burns.

Stoddard, R. H.   Literary Landmarks of Edinburgh.

Walker, H.   Three Centuries of Scottish Songs.

Wallace, William.   The Life and Works of Robert Burns, edited by Robert Chambers, revised by William Wallace.   4 vols. (with full biography and essay on Character and Genius of Burns).   For a review of this recent work and of the Centenary edition see an article in the *Scottish Review*, April, 1897, by James Davidson, entitled "New Light on Burns."

CARLYLE.

Helpful short accounts are John Nichol's *Thomas Carlyle* (English Men of Letters), Richard Garnett's *Life of Thomas Carlyle* (Great Writers), H. C. Macpherson's *Thomas Carlyle* (Famous Scots Series), and A. H. Guernsey's *Thomas Carlyle* (Appleton's Handy Volume Series).   Those interested in the subject will enjoy Flügel's little book on *Thomas Carlyle's Moral and Religious Development*, translated from the German by J. G. Tyler.   Mr. J. A. Froude has been considered Carlyle's biographer, but Professor Norton says: "To exhibit completely the extent and quality of the divergence of Mr. Froude's narrative from the truth, the whole story would have to be rewritten." This work Mr. David Wilson is now doing.   Meanwhile he has published his *Mr. Froude and Carlyle*, for, he says, "there are delusions current which must be demolished before any truthful biographer can hope for a hearing."   For Froude's Carlyle we shall soon be able to substitute Carlyle's Carlyle.

Chronological List of Carlyle's Works.

Translations, and Life of Schiller	1824–1827
French Revolution	1837
Sartor Resartus	1838
Critical and Miscellaneous Essays	1839
Chartism	1840
Heroes, Hero-Worship, and the Heroic in History	1841

ANNOUNCEMENTS